The Blues: A Very Short Introduction

Very Short Introductions available now:

For more information visit our web site
www.oup.co.uk/general/vsi/

Elijah Wald

THE BLUES

A Very Short Introduction

OXFORD
UNIVERSITY PRESS

OXFORD
UNIVERSITY PRESS

Oxford University Press, Inc., publishes works that further
Oxford University's objective of excellence
in research, scholarship, and education.

Oxford   New York
Auckland   Cape Town   Dar es Salaam   Hong Kong   Karachi
Kuala Lumpur   Madrid   Melbourne   Mexico City   Nairobi
New Delhi   Shanghai   Taipei   Toronto

With offices in
Argentina   Austria   Brazil   Chile   Czech Republic   France   Greece
Guatemala   Hungary   Italy   Japan   Poland   Portugal   Singapore
South Korea   Switzerland   Thailand   Turkey   Ukraine   Vietnam

Published by Oxford University Press, Inc.
198 Madison Avenue, New York, NY 10016

www.oup.com

Oxford is a registered trademark of Oxford University Press

Library of Congress Cataloging-in-Publication Data
Wald, Elijah.
The blues : a very short introduction / Elijah Wald.
p.   cm.
Includes bibliographical references and index.
ISBN 978-0-19-539893-9 (pbk.)
1. Blues (Music)—History and criticism.   I. Title.
ML3521.W33 2010
781.643—dc22
2010010475

1 3 5 7 9 8 6 4 2

Printed in Great Britain
by Ashford Colour Press Ltd., Gosport, Hants.
on acid-free paper

Contents

List of illustrations

Introduction

What is blues?

Blues music first swept the United States in the early 1910s, remained a driving force in the pop mainstream for some six decades, and continues to be played and heard around the world. Once performed by neighborhood bands, street corner guitarists, and theatrical divas, blues is now routinely heard as background music for car commercials and Westerns, in forms ranging from gentle acoustic guitar melodies to crunching blues-rock. Blues has been whispered, shouted, growled, moaned, and yodeled, and played on everything from harmonicas to synthesizers. So, considering a century's worth of shifting audiences, tastes, and technologies, any attempt to understand the music has to start with the question: What, exactly, is blues?

In 1917 an Irish American musical comedy star named Marie Cahill sang, "The blues ain't nothing but a good man feeling bad." Twenty-five years later, an African American guitarist named Son House sang, "The blues ain't nothing but a low-down, aching chill." In between, one of the biggest stars of the first blues recording boom, Ida Cox, sang that the blues was nothing but "your lover on your mind" and "a slow aching heart disease." All of those answers were echoed over the years by other singers and they continue to represent the broadest definition of blues, as music that expresses a universal emotion. In this sense, the word has been associated with mournful, heartrending songs in many languages and styles: *flamenco* is often described as Spanish Gypsy blues, *rembetika* as Greek blues, *morna* as Cape Verdean blues, *tango* as Argentine blues, *enka* as Japanese blues. The range of comparisons gives a sense of how deeply blues has become part of our musical understanding.

However hallowed by history, though, the idea that blues is fundamentally a musical heart-cry has some problems. For one thing, along with some of the most moving, cathartic music on earth, the American blues tradition has produced thousands of comical party songs and upbeat dance music. The first music to be called blues seems to have been slow, but not necessarily sad—it was a sexy rhythm, popular with African American working-class dancers in New Orleans and other parts of the Deep South. Once the style became a national craze in the 1910s, blues compositions were played in all sorts of tempos and rhythms, and that range has been increasing ever since. Blues continues to be associated with deeply emotional performances, but it has never been limited to them.

There is also a purely musical definition of blues: a progression of chords consisting of four bars of the tonic (I), two bars of the subdominant (IV), two bars of the tonic (I), a bar of the dominant seventh (V^7), a bar of the subdominant (IV), and two final bars of the tonic (I). This "twelve-bar blues" is what a musician means if she calls for her bandmates to play, say, "a blues in F."

This twelve-bar blues is ideally suited to the West African tradition of call-and-response, in which a lead voice or instrument states a phrase that is answered by other voices or players. In the most common twelve-bar song pattern, the leader sings two repeated lines, each of which is answered by an instrumental phrase, then a rhyming third line that is answered by a final

1. Early definitions of the blues are listed in an advertisement for Ida Cox's hit song "Blues Ain't Nothin' Else But."

instrumental passage. The Bessie Smith–Louis Armstrong duet of "St. Louis Blues" is a classic example of this sort of musical conversation:

> Smith begins by singing, "*I hate to see the evening sun go down.*"
> Armstrong echoes her final note on his cornet and adds a relaxed melodic response.
> Smith repeats, "*I hate to see the evening sun go down.*"
> Armstrong plays a series of slow, drawn-out notes.
> Smith completes the thought: "*It makes me think I'm on my last go 'round.*"
> And Armstrong builds an arching obbligato leading into the next verse.

This basic chord progression, simple as it is, has been used in many and varied contexts: the Victor Military Band playing "Memphis Blues" in 1914, Blind Lemon Jefferson singing "Matchbox Blues" in 1927, Glenn Miller swinging through "In the Mood" in 1939, Hank Williams and the Driftin' Cowboys wailing "Move It On Over" in 1947, Chuck Berry rocking through "Roll Over, Beethoven" in 1956, James Brown getting funky with "Papa's Got a Brand New Bag" in 1965, and the White Stripes grinding out "Stop Breaking Down" in the twenty-first century.

Similarly, that basic lyrical form—two repeated lines followed by a rhyming third—has been used for innumerable songs and produced some of the most memorable verses in the English language: "See, see rider, see what you done done (2x) / You made me love you, now your gal done come." "You don't know, you don't know my mind (2x) / When you see me laughin', I'm laughin' just to keep from cryin'." Or, in another mood, "Good golly, Miss Molly, sure like to ball (2x) / When you're rockin' and rollin', can't hear your mama call."

The twelve-bar/three-line pattern is the most common blues form, but once again does not fully define the style. For one thing, there are at least two other common blues chord patterns, the

4

eight- and sixteen-bar blues. The eight-bar blues may well have predated the twelve-bar, since it is a simpler form that often has just two lyrical lines: One famous early verse went, "I walked all the way from East St. Louis / Didn't have but one lousy dime." Furthermore, some blues artists—notably John Lee Hooker and Robert Pete Williams—have refused to be tied to any set chord patterns, improvising words and music as the mood struck them and varying chords and bar-lengths from verse to verse.

The basic twelve-bar form has also been used to back lyrical forms other than the two-plus-one-line verse. Some early blues verses just repeated a single line three times. Some very popular records of the 1920s and '30s, such as Papa Charlie Jackson's "Shake that Thing," divided the standard chord pattern into a two-line, four-bar verse followed by a three-line, eight-bar chorus:

> Old Uncle Jack, the jellyroll king,
> He just got tight from shaking that thing.
>> Want you to shake that thing,
>> Oh, shake that thing,
>> I'm getting sick and tired of telling you to shake that thing.

So, as with the definition that ties blues to deep emotions, the definitions that tie it to specific musical or lyrical patterns are useful in many situations, but insufficient in others.

Another common way to define blues is as a tradition that employs a range of tonal and rhythmic practices originating in West Africa. To the extent that they can be expressed in European notation, many blues melodies are based on a pentatonic or five-note "blues scale" that is frequently used by West African performers, consisting of the first, the flatted third, the fourth, the fifth, and the flatted seventh notes of the European major scale—the flatted third and seventh notes in particular are often called "blue notes." As with any description that uses formal European terms to describe non-European styles, this is a simplification:

any good blues singer uses a broad range of microtones and moves between them with a freedom and subtlety that cannot be captured in Western notation. Many of the most popular blues instruments—the slide guitar, the harmonica, the saxophone, and the standard guitar as played by note-bending virtuosos like Lonnie Johnson and B. B. King—are favored specifically because they can play those "in-between" tones.

Musicians who demonstrate a mastery of those microtones and a similarly African-derived rhythmic sense are often said to have a "blues feel." In practice, though, such descriptions tend to be a mix of musical judgments and judgments of cultural authenticity. Many people consider the blues tradition to be primarily a matter of ethnicity and culture, the musical heritage of the African American South, which can rarely if ever be fully understood by northern, or foreign, or white artists. In a similar sense the word is sometimes applied to the literary style of African American poets and novelists—or, more rarely, European American writers who are familiar with African American milieus—whose work reflects the language and spirit of the world that produced blues music.

Finally, there is the most widely understood definition of blues in day-to-day speech, which is as a marketing category. The range of performers who have been marketed as blues artists is huge and disparate, and the decisions that have resulted in some being filed as blues while others are filed as folk, jazz, or rock are full of odd contradictions. For example, Jimi Hendrix is typically filed as a rocker, but Stevie Ray Vaughan's covers of Hendrix are typically filed as blues. (A cover is a recording that deliberately recreates another artist's performance of the same song.) Nonetheless, most listeners have a pretty good idea of which records are likely to be filed in blues sections of stores and played on blues radio shows, and which performers are likely to be presented at blues festivals. And, despite its logical shortcomings, this definition reflects the evolving history of blues as a commercial style, and is no more vague or contradictory than the equally market-based definitions of jazz, rock, or classical music.

So, depending on the situation, one can define blues in emotional, musical, cultural, or commercial terms, and these definitions overlap at times and diverge at others. Blues has meant many different things to many different people over the years, and no definition will ever satisfy all listeners or readers. The best one can hope to do in a short introduction is to provide a selective overview of how blues and our understanding of blues have evolved, and to provide some guideposts for further exploration— while always remembering that there are other, equally valid ways to cover the same territory. No single book can touch on more than a few aspects of blues, or give more than a hint of how this apparently simple style has managed to permeate virtually every other form of American music and influence so many other styles around the world.

Part I
A short history of blues

Chapter 1
Roots of the blues

The history of blues as a broadly popular style of music begins in the fall of 1912, when W. C. Handy's "Memphis Blues"—along with two similar songs, "Dallas Blues" and "Baby Seals Blues"—sparked a national craze. Handy was a music teacher, bandleader, and songwriter based in Memphis, Tennessee, and he modeled his blues on older songs he had heard around the Mississippi Delta region. "Memphis Blues" was not the first blues to be published in sheet music form, but its lively melody caught the ear of a New York bandleader named James Reese Europe, who was then employed by America's most influential dance instructors, Vernon and Irene Castle. The Castles used "Memphis Blues" to accompany a new step called the fox trot, and this helped to make the song into an enduring hit. In 1914 it became the first blues preserved on record, in an instrumental version by the Victor Military Band and then by a white vaudeville singer named Morton Harvey. Handy capitalized on his success by writing a follow-up, "St. Louis Blues," which included a section in tango rhythm—another specialty of the Castles—and the next few years brought so many blues hits that by 1917 Marion Harris, who sometimes billed herself as the "Queen of the Blues," was making fun of the fad, singing "Everybody's Crazy 'Bout the Dog-gone Blues, But I'm Happy." (The lyric began in classic fashion: "Blues ain't nothing but the easy-going heart disease.")

Though most of the people listening and dancing to blues seem to have thought of it as a new style, it was also associated with older rural and street music—one of Handy's biggest hits referred to "the blind man on the corner who sings the Beale Street blues." So any understanding of blues has to begin with some exploration of its sources in the earlier music of the African American South.

Folk songs

The folk music of black southerners—which is to say, the music nonprofessionals played and sang for their own pleasure and shared with their friends and neighbors—drew on many traditions, from European and African importations to commercial pop songs and tunes people made up on the spur of the moment. Some of the most distinctive elements of what would come to be known as blues can be traced to West Africa: common rhythms, instrumental techniques that were adapted by banjo players, fiddlers, and eventually guitarists, and a rich and varied range of singing styles. The vocal traditions were particularly important, since the vast majority of black Americans had arrived in the United States as slaves, without any possessions, and most continued to be extremely poor even after emancipation. Singing is one of the few pleasures that requires nothing but a voice and can be enjoyed while alone or while working. Rhythmic work songs kept groups of laborers moving in unison, and people working alone would sing "field hollers" to calm herd animals, to let their friends and co-workers know where they were, or simply to pass the time.

The group work songs provided blues with one of its most common features, the widespread African practice known as "call and response." A lead vocalist sings a line, and the people around him reply, either echoing his words or singing a responsive phrase. In the Americas, such songs were adapted to group labor on plantations, and later on railroads, lumber gangs, and sailing ships—many popular "sea shanties," sung by black and white

2. A Louisiana singer nicknamed Stavin' Chain sings a murder ballad with fiddle accompaniment.

sailors alike, have roots in this tradition. In blues, this call and response is typically refigured as a conversation between a singer and an instrument, either played by another musician—as in Bessie Smith's duets with Louis Armstrong—or by the singer on her own piano, guitar, or harmonica.

Meanwhile, the "field hollers" or "moans" provided blues with distinctive vocal textures. (The terms "holler" and "moan" are more or less interchangeable, though the former is more common when describing outdoor singing, and the latter for home or church styles.) To a great extent, these were simply vocal improvisations, and many people did not even think of them as songs: Muddy Waters recalled that in the fields of the Mississippi Delta, "Every man would be hollering, but you didn't pay that no mind.... They was just made-up things. Like a feller be workin' or most likely some gal be workin' near and you want to say somethin' to 'em. So you holler it." Such hollers could be wordless, moaning melodies; scraps of songs remembered from minstrel shows, dances, or church; or improvised meditations on the singer's feelings. For example, one of the most beautiful surviving hollers—which the folklorist Alan Lomax preserved and titled "Tangle Eye Blues"—is the lament of a prisoner named Walter "Tangle Eye" Jackson, recorded at the Mississippi State Penitentiary in 1947:

> Well, it must have been the devil that foo-ooled me he-ee-ere,
> Hey-ey, hey, hey-ey,

Jackson's voice soars and dips, stretching his phrases into supple, floating cries.

> Whoa, I'm all down and ow-ow-ow-ow-out,
> Hey-ey, ey, ooooh, o-oh, Lord."

Countless blues singers have built their songs in a similar way, fitting their thoughts to scraps of melody and filling the spaces between their words with vocal or instrumental passages that extended the mood. Lomax called Jackson's holler a "blues" not because it followed any particular blues form but because its theme and style reminded him of the songs of stars like Bessie Smith and Blind Lemon Jefferson. Lomax was particularly interested in such hollers because he saw them as a link between the African past and later blues and gospel; on an album released in the 1970s he emphasized this connection by intercutting a Mississippi holler with a similarly moaning, melismatic vocal from Senegal, the two performances blending into a single intercontinental lament.

Religious songs

The title of "Tangle Eye Blues" places it in a secular tradition, but its words could as easily be understood as the lament of a Christian led astray by the devil. And although black Americans have often been as judgmental as their white neighbors when it comes to separating religious music and party music, a great deal of black church singing draws on the same sources and has undergone the same evolution as blues and other secular styles. The call-and-response forms of the work songs were also used for camp-meeting spirituals and gospel compositions, and the loose meter and microtonal inflections of the field hollers can still be heard in the moaning of many black religious congregations.

African American church music also drew on other influences, though, in particular the hymns of composers such as the seventeenth-century English theologian Isaac Watts. In 1842 a white minister named Charles Colcock Jones wrote: "One great advantage in teaching [the Negroes] good psalms and hymns, is that they are thereby induced to lay aside the extravagant and nonsensical chants, and catches and hallelujah songs of their own composing; and when they sing, which is very often while about their business or of an evening in their houses, they will have something profitable to sing." But singers did not necessarily have to choose between what they learned from hymnals and what they learned from their neighbors; many were comfortable with both styles and combined them, reworking European harmonies and the ornate language of the King James Bible to fit with African-derived forms. Such interchanges have continued over the years, with African American religious music drawing on secular styles and African American secular performers taking tunes and techniques from the churches, to the point that the distinction between sacred and secular—important as it is to many people, both black and white—often has little meaning in terms of musical approach or of the way listeners react to performances that thrill or move them.

Professional styles

Though often celebrated as a folk or "roots" style, from the beginning blues also drew on music performed by professional and semi-professional entertainers. The distinction between folk and professional (or "pop") styles is not always clear: Professional "singing school" teachers spread church songs that have survived in oral tradition, and field hollers and blues have reworked lines drawn from pop songs, while old folk lyrics and melodies have been adapted and published by both gospel and pop composers. By the same token, although blues has deep roots in older styles and continues to be sung by nonprofessionals, the style that emerged in the 1910s and '20s was largely created by professional entertainers and greeted by audiences as a modern pop trend.

Of course, what is new to one audience may be old to another. W. C. Handy and Ma Rainey, who were separately advertised as the Father and Mother of the Blues, were up-to-date entertainers, but Handy recalled being inspired by the music of a ragged guitarist he heard at a Mississippi Delta train depot in 1903, and Rainey said that she learned her first blues—though the style did not yet have that name—from a girl who came to hear her sing in a tent show in rural Missouri in 1902. In the words of the folklorist John W. Work, who interviewed Rainey in the 1920s: "The song was so strange and poignant...[and] elicited such a response from the audiences that it won a special place in her act. Many times she was asked what kind of song it was, and one day she replied, in a moment of inspiration, 'It's the *Blues*.'"

Handy and Rainey were both veterans of the "minstrel show" circuit. Minstrelsy took its name from a quartet of white entertainers who made their debut in New York in 1843 as the Virginia Minstrels and purported to be presenting music and dances they had adapted from slaves in the South. For the sake of verisimilitude they colored their hands and faces black, and their success inspired a flock of "blackface minstrel" imitators. By the 1850s there were also some African American minstrel troupes performing similar material, and in the early twentieth century such groups toured throughout the country, and were especially popular in the rural South.

The standard minstrel show included banjo and fiddle players, singers, and comedians who played tambourine and bones (literally a pair of polished bones, which the player clicked together like castanets). As fashions changed, other instruments were added, and much minstrel music ceased to be linked to plantation traditions. Minstrel troupes performed everything from opera and sentimental "parlor songs" to comic novelties and dance music. In areas without formal theaters, minstrel shows often provided the largest and best-organized musical entertainment available, and virtually any African American star who wanted to reach a broad audience did minstrel tours. As Handy wrote, "It goes without saying that minstrels were a disreputable lot in the eyes of a large section of upper-crust Negroes...but it was also true that all the best talent of that generation came down the same drain. The composers, the singers, the musicians, the speakers, the stage performers—the minstrel shows got them all."

Like the blackface makeup—which was routinely used by both Euro- and Afro-American minstrel comedians into the 1940s— many minstrel songs and routines were at best stereotypical and at worst blatantly racist. But that did not keep them from being laughed at by plenty of black audiences, and minstrel material regularly resurfaced on the blues scene. Large African American minstrel companies like Silas Green from New Orleans and the Rabbit's Foot Minstrels (in which Rainey starred for many years) toured all over the South, and similar material was also presented in the smaller, less formal "medicine shows." Medicine shows ranged from two or three people to fairly large troupes, with the entertainment designed to draw a crowd that could be persuaded to buy some dubious medicine or ointment. Many rural musicians, both white and black, traveled with such shows, as well as in circuses and, more rarely, on the vaudeville theater circuits.

Minstrelsy and its offshoots were far from the only professional styles to cross racial boundaries; virtually all southern rural music shows signs of Afro-European interchange. The "square dances" popular throughout the South were adapted from French ballroom figures, but the music that was played for them mixed Irish and African fiddle techniques. Fiddles of various kinds are as common in Africa as in Europe, and some experts have estimated that between a third and a half of the southeastern fiddle repertoire is of African American origin. The other standard rural instrument, the banjo, was originally an African import, which became popular with both races because it was loud, portable, and easier to make than a fiddle or guitar—the basic banjo was just an animal skin stretched over a wooden hoop, with another piece of wood attached as a neck.

African-derived tunes and techniques crossed racial lines not only because they were catchy but because such a large proportion of the music performed in the antebellum South was played by African Americans. The minstrel craze typed slave musicians as playing banjos and fiddles, but they also played pianos, cellos, flutes, and whatever else was demanded by white listeners, and their repertoire ranged from their own melodies to European classical compositions. The more formal concert music left little trace in blues, but well into the twentieth century many black rural guitarists still played "Spanish Fandango," the standard beginning piece in nineteenth-century classical guitar manuals. Meanwhile, white musicians and dancers were adopting African American approaches, to the point that it is often impossible to trace a given style or tune specifically to African or European sources.

Many rural musicians were farmers who picked up spare money or groceries by playing at weekend dances, but others were full-time professionals who could perform anything from fiddle tunes to ragtime, Tin Pan Alley waltzes, and, in some cases, classical concert pieces. Isolated communities developed regional styles and specialties that would influence their local variations of blues, but after emancipation African Americans began traveling widely in search of better jobs and living conditions, so songs and styles spread rapidly across the South and then to northern industrial centers that drew large populations of southern immigrants.

The turn of the twentieth century was a particularly rich period of musical innovation, due not only to this mobility but to the dawn of recording and the increased availability of store-bought instruments. Sears Roebuck's mail order business made guitars accessible to musicians who previously had considered them an upper-class instrument, and the shift from banjo to guitar played a significant role in the rise of blues: Banjos have very fast sound decay, which means that one has to play relatively quickly and cannot mimic the drawn-out contours of a vocal performance. The guitar has greater sustain, making it more appropriate for slow songs, and also has a warmer tone, making it more suitable for accompanying sentimental ballads or moaning hollers.

Records were meanwhile making a previously unimaginable range of music available even to remote rural households—though until the 1920s, very few of those records preserved African American or rural performances. A handful of African Americans were recorded as early as the 1890s—the musical comedian Bert Williams was a major recording star in the second decade of the twentieth century—but their records were marketed to a mainstream (which is to say, mostly white), middle-class audience and tailored to that audience's tastes. And when blues hit in the teens, the early records were aimed at similar audiences and featured white bands and artists. Like the blackface minstrels, many of these white blues interpreters claimed to have adapted their material from African American folk sources, and it is similarly hard to sort out how much of this was true and how much was marketing. Both minstrelsy and blues clearly drew on older African American rural traditions, but in both cases professional compositions were also being imitated by rural amateurs, who in turn were imitated by the next generation of professionals—and semi-professionals, and semi-amateurs. As a result, by the time blues reached the national market it was impossible to sort out to what extent the style had been formed by unknown bards in rural cabins and on small-town street corners, and to what extent it had been developed by professional entertainers in tent and theater shows.

Chapter 2
Prewar blues

By 1920 most Americans were familiar with blues songs, but no one seems to have considered blues a musical genre in anything like the modern sense. Blues were performed by vaudeville stars, blackface minstrels, street musicians, ragtime orchestras, and in particular by the new wave of jazz bands. (The first jazz hit was the Original Dixieland Jazz Band's 1917 recording of "Livery Stable Blues," a twelve-bar blues instrumental with novelty animal imitations.) Some bands were known for their sexy blues tempos and sultry blue moans, and some singers specialized in the style, including the Afro-American artists Ma Rainey, Bessie Smith, and Ethel Waters, and the Euro-American artists Marion Harris and Al Bernard. But all of those bands and artists also performed other material, and the only people who were devoting their careers exclusively to blues were a few songwriters. W. C. Handy was the most successful of these, and during the teens he moved from Memphis to New York and formed a publishing company called Pace and Handy, which encouraged other composers to produce blues material.

It was records, though, that made blues a dominant force in the African American entertainment business and the model for later pop trends from R&B to hip-hop. By the late teens, record companies had discovered that discs tailored to the tastes of ethnic communities—Italians, Poles, and speakers of

Spanish or Yiddish—could provide lucrative sidelines. A black composer-publisher named Perry Bradford was convinced that African Americans would be equally willing to buy records made specifically for them. At first he met with little encouragement from the record labels. Since the logic of segregation was that black and white audiences attended different theaters but wanted the same kinds of acts, the label managers assumed that black customers would be happy to hear their favorite songs performed by white superstars like Sophie Tucker.

Bradford persisted, though, and early in 1920 he persuaded the OKeh company to take a chance on a Harlem theater singer named Mamie Smith. She recorded a couple of his songs with a white orchestra, and the record did well enough that OKeh let her go back into the studio with a group of African American accompanists and perform a Bradford composition called "Crazy Blues." To the industry's astonishment, it became one of the biggest-selling discs of the year, and the blues recording boom was on.

Early blues queens and the rise of "race records"

The success of "Crazy Blues" set off a new era in popular music. By the end of 1921 Smith had been joined by other African American singers, including Ethel Waters, Lucille Hegamin, Alberta Hunter, and Edith Wilson. The record companies were still a bit confused about what they were selling, billing Waters as "The Best Blues Singer in America," Smith as "The Greatest Race Phonograph Star," and Hegamin as "The Celebrated Colored Contralto." But today all of these singers are remembered as "blues queens," and they established a female dynasty so pervasive that the most popular black male singer to record blues in the early 1920s, Charles Anderson, was a female impersonator.

The first blues queens were versatile theater and cabaret singers. They recorded blues because that was what the record companies

CRAZY BLUES

By PERRY BRADFORD

MAMIE SMITH AND HER JAZZ HOUNDS

Get this number for your phonograph on Okeh Record No. 4169

PUBLISHED BY
PERRY BRADFORD
MUSIC PUB. CO.
1547 BROADWAY, N. Y. C.

3. Sheet music for the breakthrough "Race" recording "Crazy Blues,"
featuring Mamie Smith accompanied by her Jazz Hounds, including
the Harlem stride pianist Willie "The Lion" Smith.

wanted but were equally comfortable performing the Tin Pan
Alley pop numbers favored by their white counterparts. Waters
was somewhat exceptional, having started out as a blues specialist
in the teens, but she also developed a mainstream pop career, and

her style was much gentler than that of the southern tent-show singers. In her autobiography, she recalled that when she started working in black vaudeville the patrons greeted her as a novel contrast to "shouters" like Bessie Smith and Ma Rainey. "I would sing 'St. Louis Blues,' but very softly. It was the first time that kind of Negro audience ever let my kind of low singing get by."

The early African American blues record queens arguably sounded as much like Sophie Tucker and Marion Harris as they did like Rainey and Smith, but their success proved that there was a viable market for recordings by African Americans. By 1923 numerous record labels had separate Race catalogs—"Race" being that era's respectful synonym for "colored" or "Negro." Not all black artists were relegated to the Race series; if a record seemed likely to appeal to white listeners, it was released in the standard pop catalog. But for the first time African American music was being viewed as a separate genre, and African Americans were being targeted as consumers with their own tastes and preferences. Among other things, that meant that black music was becoming disassociated from minstrelsy, and black stars were singing about their own lives, in their own voices, without using dialect or stereotyped comedy.

Given the extent to which blues dominated the Race record market, it was only a matter of time before producers sought out the singers who had established the style on the southern circuit. Bessie Smith released her first record for Columbia in May 1923, and it had almost as profound an effect as "Crazy Blues." Smith had at times included Tin Pan Alley material in her shows, but blues was her meat. She had the relaxed inflections of the Deep South, the control of an opera diva, the phrasing of a jazz soloist, and the emotional power of a great actress. From her first release ("Down Hearted Blues" backed with "Gulf Coast Blues") she was acclaimed as the greatest blues singer on records, and soon she was appearing on radio programs and touring in northern theaters. Record company scouts sought out other southerners who shared her moaning, soulful sound, signing up Clara Smith (no relation to either Mamie or Bessie), Ida Cox, Sippie Wallace— and Ma Rainey, who made her record debut in 1924, after more than twenty years as a touring star.

The southern blues queens were masters of what Robert Palmer would dub the "deep blues" style: vocal timbres, tonal subtleties, and a rhythmic sense reflecting older African American folk traditions. Their repertoires overlapped what their northern counterparts had been recording—three of Bessie Smith's first ten records were covers of Alberta Hunter hits, including the classic "Tain't Nobody's Business if I Do." But they also knew songs that were unlike anything in the mainstream pop market and reflected a vastly different range of experiences. These songs were not necessarily new: Jelly Roll Morton, who was born around 1890, recalled that one of the first blues he heard as a child in New Orleans lamented the hard life of a street prostitute, and many of Smith's and Rainey's lyrics undoubtedly reached back to the same period. But nothing like them had appeared in the mainstream pop market, and although the blues queens wore gorgeous gowns and appeared in the most prominent black theaters, they were far from typical pop stars. Their records sold to white customers as well as black, but their core audience was African American women—whether in the South or in the growing ghettos of the urban North and Midwest—and they sang about that audience's concerns.

Those concerns ranged from economic hardships to travel and crime, but by far the most common topic was romantic and sexual relationships, which the blues queens treated in a way that still seems startlingly modern. Mainstream pop favored romantic dreams, but blues dealt with the sorrows and joys of real relationships: cheating, abandonment, and abuse were balanced by exuberant physical pleasure. As Angela Davis has pointed out, the freedoms to travel and to choose one's sexual partners had typically been denied under slavery—which was within the living memory of some blues listeners—and the blues queens celebrated those freedoms in no uncertain terms: "No time to marry, no time to settle down," Bessie Smith sang, "I'm a young woman, and ain't done running 'round." And if their current lives still involved trials and troubles, blues provided a way to speak out: Smith threatened that if her man interfered with her affairs, "I'm like the butcher right down the street, I can cut you all to pieces like I would a piece of meat."

Ma Rainey sang of the harsh realities of domestic violence, describing a man who would "take all my money, blacken both of my eyes, give it to another woman, come home and tell me lies." But she also sang about finding happiness in lesbian culture, dressing up in "a collar and a tie" to go out with "a crowd of my friends / They must have been women, 'cause I don't like no men."

Rainey's work also reflected her many years touring the rural South. She sang about moonshine whiskey and the boll weevils that were destroying cotton crops, and although most of her records featured small jazz ensembles, she also recorded with rurally identified instruments: banjos, guitars, and jug bands.

Rural southern music had begun finding its own record market shortly after the beginning of the Race music boom. In 1923 an OKeh scout who had gone to Atlanta to record a couple of local blues queens cut a record by a scratchy-sounding white violinist and singer named Fiddlin' John Carson. Carson's first release—a nineteenth-century minstrel song called "Little Old Log Cabin"— became a surprise hit, and soon several companies were selling discs aimed at white rural southerners.

Until Carson's success, record promoters had assumed that country folk listened to scratchy fiddles and plunking banjos rather than to pianos and brass bands for the same reason they used horse-drawn wagons rather than automobiles: because they could not afford anything better. In the blues field, that meant that as the market expanded from white vaudeville stars to black vaudeville stars to southern tent-show stars, it was still taken for granted that buyers wanted to hear the top touring professionals. Carson's success proved that, on the contrary, a lot of people preferred their local music, including artists who would have been laughed off the stage of an urban theater. As the rural southern market grew, records ceased to simply mirror the national music scene and began featuring regional performers and styles that did not fit the familiar show business paradigms.

In the fall of 1923, OKeh recorded Sarah Martin accompanied by a guitarist named Sylvester Weaver and advertised the result as "the first blue guitar record," with a drawing of an old black man strumming in front of a country shack—and lest there be any doubt what market was being targeted, her next record added a note that customers could "order by mail from Down Home in Georgia." The following summer Paramount presented "Papa Charlie Jackson—the famous Blues-singing-Guitar-playing Man. Only man living who sings, self-accompanied, for Blues records," adding that "this man Charlie can sing and play the blues even better than a woman can." In fact, Jackson played a six-string banjo, and a blues guitarist-singer named Ed Andrews had recorded previously—nor was Jackson any threat to Bessie Smith or Ma Rainey as a singer. But he had a jaunty, infectious style, and his most influential record was a new kind of twelve-bar hit: a risqué ragtime dance number titled "Shake that Thing."

Jackson's music combined the appeals of blues, minstrelsy, and country music, and although he was from New Orleans and lived in Chicago, his records seem to have been particularly popular with rural southern listeners, both black and white. By contrast, the next male blues record star, a New Orleanian named Lonnie Johnson, had a hip, modern appeal, with crooning vocals and intricate, jazzy guitar. Musically, the two men were opposites: Jackson's mix of banjo and comedy harked back to minstrelsy, while Johnson was comfortable sitting in with Louis Armstrong and Duke Ellington and shaped the urban style that would dominate blues in the 1930s. Nonetheless, both sounded like adept showbiz professionals. A specifically rural-sounding blues style did not reach a mass audience until 1926, with the first recordings of a blind Texas street singer named Lemon Jefferson.

Country blues

When Jelly Roll Morton recalled visiting Houston, Texas, in the early teens, he said "there wasn't any decent music around there, only Jew's harps, harmonicas, mandolins, guitars, and fellows singing the spasmodic blues—sing awhile, and pick awhile till they thought of another word to say." From a literate musician like Morton that was severe criticism, and most theater managers and record producers shared his tastes. But by the mid-1920s it was becoming clear that a lot of listeners had other standards. Blind Lemon Jefferson was exactly the kind of player Morton disparaged, but he drew big crowds on the streets of Dallas's black neighborhoods, and a local store manager wrote to Paramount Records that customers would be eager to hear him on record. Jefferson's discs sold spectacularly, not only across the rural South but in the industrial Midwest, and heralded a brief golden age of rural blues recording.

Jefferson was about the same age as Bessie Smith, and some ten years younger than Ma Rainey, but he sounded like their country grandfather. His vocals had the soaring, moaning quality of the field hollers, and he played guitar with a jerky, anarchic virtuosity unlike anything on record. Most of his songs were based on the standard twelve-bar form, but performed with the "spasmodic" freedom Morton decried, stretching a bar to wring more feeling from it or cutting it short to create excitement.

Jefferson's success inspired record companies to take chances on other street, medicine show, and "juke joint" entertainers, and many historians regard the years from 1926 until the Depression arrived in 1929 as the richest period of blues recording. Though the most frequently recorded artists tended to be based in urban locations—Jefferson in Dallas; Blind Willie McTell and Peg Leg Howell in Atlanta; and Frank Stokes, Jim Jackson, Gus Cannon's Jug Stompers, and the Memphis Jug Band in Memphis—their sound drew on older rural traditions, and their records were particularly popular in the countryside. Many of their songs predated the blues boom, and along with minstrel and vaudeville material they played styles that reached back to the roots of African American music.

Indeed, although their records appeared later, many scholars treat the early "country blues" artists as representing the roots of commercial stars such as Rainey and Handy. This is a tricky argument, since it is hard to say how accurately recordings made in the later 1920s reflect earlier traditions. The breadth of rural styles represented on those records, and the fact that numerous songs were common throughout the South, indicate that they were tapping deep sources, but the rural bluesmen had grown up during the heyday of vaudeville blues and were clearly influenced by current trends. It is always tempting to equate rural music with old-fashioned music, but although Jefferson and his peers recycled older material and techniques, they were also forging new approaches to blues. While the white rural market was geared to nostalgia, advertising records as "Old Time," few African Americans treasured memories of "good old days," especially in the slave-era South. So although Jefferson was marketed as "down home," and some of his songs were derived from field hollers and country dance tunes, he devoted the overwhelming majority of his records to material that reflected the commercial blues craze. His most influential song, "Matchbox Blues," popularized an image that had first appeared in one of Rainey's lyrics and would be recycled by everyone from Billie Holiday to Sam Cooke, Carl Perkins, and the Beatles: "I'm sitting here wondering, will a matchbox hold my clothes / I ain't got so many matches, but I've got so far to go."

Jefferson's success opened the Race record market to a dazzlingly idiosyncratic range of stylists. Though the great blues queens each had unique talents, they shared a common vocal approach, similar accompaniments (frequently by the same musicians), and overlapping material—when Bessie Smith hit with a cover of Alberta Hunter's "Down Hearted Blues," it inspired further covers by blues queens on eight different record labels. By contrast, the down home artists who recorded in Jefferson's wake often bore no resemblance to one another beyond the fact that they did not sound like anyone in mainstream show business. Blind Blake, Jefferson's first major rival at Paramount, had a light, conversational voice that was utterly unlike Jefferson's street-tempered shout, and his playing recalled ragtime piano (ads celebrated his "piano-sounding guitar"). In later years, the blues scholar Bruce Bastin would dub this ragtime-flavored guitar approach "Piedmont blues," reflecting its popularity in Georgia and Carolinas, and it is often contrasted with the more rhythmically propulsive and complex playing of players in northern Mississippi.

Their do-it-yourself accompaniments and identifiably regional styles set all of these artists apart from the vaudeville divas and dance bands. Nonetheless, like the urban professionals they were comfortable with plenty of non-blues material, and at least some of them seem to have recorded blues largely at the behest of the record scouts. Jefferson was at his best singing blues, but Blake seemed at least equally at home with comic ragtime numbers. Willie McTell was particularly versatile, comfortable with blues, ragtime, hillbilly ballads, sentimental parlor songs, pop hits, and rambling comic monologues.

This breadth of material was recorded not only because it suited the performers' talents and tastes but also because the record companies could not predict what their audiences might buy. Though some down-home, guitar-backed records were directed at the same audience that was buying Smith and Rainey, others clearly appealed to fans of older ragtime and rural dance styles, or provided rawer sounds to suit the rowdy young denizens of rural juke joints.

The country blues performers have been far more popular with modern listeners than the blues queens—in large part because they are now heard as forerunners of rock 'n' roll—so it is worth emphasizing that throughout the 1920s women with jazz bands continued to be the biggest stars in the blues field. Jefferson, Blake, and their peers sold well on records, but they never headlined in the major black theaters. Meanwhile, even after the blues queens had virtually ceased recording, they remained popular live performers—as late as the mid-1930s, Ida Cox was leading a troupe of two dozen singers and musicians. With that caveat in mind, though, the influence of the country bluesmen on later styles gives them a special importance. And if the attention paid to them by modern critics and historians would have astounded their original fans, it is justified by the variety of their musical approaches, both as individual creative artists and as representatives of broad regional styles.

Many country blues performers developed their skills within relatively small communities that had evolved unique ways of playing and singing. In the 1920s and '30s neither scholars nor fans seem to have paid much attention to regional patterns—Jefferson's records, in particular, were bought and imitated throughout the South—but later historians have tended to highlight three main areas: Texas, the Piedmont, and the Mississippi Delta. Such divisions arguably reflect recording patterns more than cultural patterns—certain regional styles are well documented because recording scouts held auditions in particular towns, and musicians then brought their friends to later sessions—but they also provide some insight into how styles were formed.

Texas's reputation as a blues center dates to the dawn of the craze. One of the first documented twelve-bar blues—almost certainly assembled from earlier, undocumented sources—was published in 1912 by a white composer named Hart Wand as "Dallas Blues," and registered for copyright that same year as "Negro Blues" by Leroy "Lasses" White, a white minstrel singer working at a Dallas theater. This song resembled some of Jefferson's work (like his "Bad Luck Blues," it uses a stuttering, repeated phrase in the first line of each verse), suggesting a process of give-and-take between theater and street corner performers on the Dallas scene. But Texas is a big state and was far from uniform in either population or culture. Most black Texans had arrived after emancipation, bringing a mix of musical styles from their previous regions, and on the vast cattle ranches, black, white, and Mexican cowboys often worked side by side and traded songs. ("Home on the Range," though apparently derived from a Victorian magazine poem, was first collected as a song from a black Texas cow-camp cook.)

As a result, although Texas has always been a major blues center, it had no single, defining style. The region's most important singers after Jefferson included Texas Alexander, who is particularly significant because—probably because he was one of the few rural blues artists who did not play an instrument—he was the only performer in this period to record pure, free-form field hollers as well as the current blues styles. (In a surprisingly effective collaboration, several of these were accompanied by Lonnie Johnson's innovative guitar improvisations.)

Another Texan, Blind Willie Johnson, played only Christian religious music and thus was not thought of as a blues singer by his original audience, but his eerily voice-like slide guitar style influenced many secular players, from Georgia's Willie McTell to Mississippi's Fred McDowell. Like Alexander, Johnson was deeply immersed in the oldest, most African-rooted rural traditions: his most popular records in the 1920s were shouted musical sermons that helped shape later gospel styles, but today his most celebrated performance is "Dark Was the Night, Cold Was the Ground," an introspective, wordless conversation between his moaning voice and guitar.

Other interesting Texans included Coley Jones, who led a ragtime dance ensemble called the Dallas String Band, and Victoria Spivey, a pianist and singer who would go on to run her own blues label and record the young Bob Dylan. In terms of regional schools, though, Texas was too large and varied to produce the sort of unified, distinctive styles that emerged in the Piedmont and the Delta.

In contrast to Texas's relatively recent migrants, the Piedmont was home to some of the most settled African American communities in the South. Since older listeners tend to prefer the music of their youth, and entertainers in settled communities needed to please both old and young customers, the successful Piedmont musicians were adept at playing the ragtime, minstrel, and country dance tunes of the previous generation, and they carried some of the same techniques and inflections into their blues work. Blind Blake was originally from Florida, but he seems to have spent most of his career around the Piedmont states, and even his most straightforward blues performances retained a ragtime flavor, while his singing had the clear diction of a comedian or ballad singer.

The most versatile of the Piedmont artists, Blind Willie McTell, combined the local style with what he was hearing on records, blending Blake's perky dance rhythms with Jefferson's lonesome cry, and ranging from smoothly danceable ragtime to Jefferson's "spasmodic" picking and slide pieces that evoked Willie Johnson. Born in rural Georgia, not far from the town he immortalized in his "Statesboro Blues," McTell spent his professional life in Atlanta, where he performed on the street and at local restaurants through the 1950s. Atlanta was one of the main urban centers of the southeast and a regular stopping place for the recording teams that came south in the 1920s, so the Atlanta players left a rich legacy on disc. McTell even changed his name to get around the exclusive contracts he signed with each company, recording as Blind Sammie for Columbia, Georgia Bill for OKeh, and Hot Shot Willie for Victor. His fellow Atlantans included Peg Leg Howell, an older singer who often recorded with the violinist Eddie Anthony and whose repertoire included fiddle hoedowns, ballads, and even a song based on the cries of a coal vendor. Among the more purely blues-focused artists, Barbecue Bob distinguished himself as a strong singer and songwriter, and like McTell demonstrated the local fashion for twelve-string guitar, the less common relative of the six-string instrument.

Another influential school of Piedmont artists was based in Greenville and Spartanburg, South Carolina. Though less well documented on early records, this group included Gary Davis and Willie Walker, two of the greatest virtuosos in the ragtime blues style. Davis devoted most of his life to religious music but also played intricate, multisection ragtime arrangements and occasional blues, and in the 1950s and '60s, after moving to New York, he became an influential and much-recorded performer and guitar teacher. Walker, by contrast, left only two songs to prove his formidable talents, and neither of them is the sort of complex ragtime piece that Davis recalled him playing—an important reminder that what survives from the 1920s and '30s is only a small and not necessarily representative sample of what was around at the time.

Blake's hip humor and catchy rhythms made him popular across the South, and Josh White, a young singer and guitarist from Greenville, carved out a niche in the early 1930s by moving to New York and making budget blues discs for a department store label. But in general the Piedmont players' ragtime inflections seem to have struck most Race record buyers as old-fashioned. The only artist from the region to attract a wide audience after the first flood of rural recording was the North Carolinian Blind Boy Fuller, and although he was a strong singer and expert player, his success was in a great part due to having some of the most comically filthy lyrics on record. So although it continued to have an audience on its home turf, the Piedmont style was not widely imitated by musicians in other regions.

Mississippi, by contrast, produced some of the most enduringly influential styles in blues, and many people consider it the music's heartland. One reason was the density of its black population: some Delta counties were more than 90 percent African American. Another was that most of those people were relative newcomers, since annual Mississippi River floods made the Delta region hard to settle and much of it was still swampland at the end of the nineteenth century. As a result, during the formative years of the blues boom the region's black population was both particularly susceptible to new musical fashions and relatively uninfluenced by white tastes.

As in other regions, it is somewhat misleading to speak of a unified Delta style. The area was home to many kinds of musicians: African American horn bands were popular in the towns and fiddle bands in the countryside. Indeed, though most of the Delta players preserved on record were guitarists, the area's most popular recording act was the Mississippi Sheiks, led by a fiddler named Lonnie Chatmon. The Sheiks were part of a musical elite that included several other Chatmons (notably Bo Chatmon, who recorded as a fiddler with various bands and as a solo guitarist-singer under the name Bo Carter) and the brothers Joe and Charlie McCoy. The Chatmons' and McCoys' recordings are overwhelmingly devoted to blues, but at live performances they were noted for their versatility: Lonnie Chatmon read musical notation and kept up with the latest sheet music hits, and Charlie McCoy made part of his living in Chicago playing Italian mandolin tunes and singing with his brother in a good-time jazz band, the Harlem Hamfats. These musicians played not only for black plantation dances but at the better-paying gigs for white customers, and their blues records were remembered and copied by white as well as black musicians.

In the long term, though, the Sheiks have been overshadowed by a guitarist and singer named Charlie Patton. According to some reports Patton was related to the Chatmons—they certainly knew each other's music—but he was not the kind of player who could reliably crank out the latest pop songs. In terms of the current trends, he was something of a musical primitive, and his original fans tended to recall his showmanship as much as his music—he would make up songs about local characters and play his guitar behind his head or between his legs. On record, though, what is most striking about Patton is his gruff, shouting voice and his astounding command of rhythm. "Down the Dirt Road Blues," from 1929, finds him drumming on damped strings, adding bass accents and descending melodic runs on the treble strings to create counter-rhythms, and providing yet another rhythmic pulse with his vocals. This polyrhythmic virtuosity has obvious roots in African drumming, and it is probably no coincidence that the hill country just east of the Delta has preserved a "fife and drum" tradition that sounds closer to its African roots than virtually any other music in the United States.

Patton's records appeared at the tail end of the country blues period and attracted relatively little attention outside the Delta, but on his home turf he inspired a school of similar players. His guitar arrangements were reworked by contemporaries including Tommy Johnson, who mixed them with a smoother vocal style and yodeling falsetto, and the duo of Son House and Willie Brown, who were popular juke joint entertainers in the plantations around Clarksdale. House was a friend of Patton's, and they traveled north together with Brown and the pianist Louise Johnson to record in Paramount's Wisconsin studio. House added biting slide guitar lines to Patton's rhythmic foundation, and his powerful playing and fervent, shouting vocals—he had been a preacher before turning to blues—would be a formative influence on two defining Delta artists of the next generation, Robert Johnson and Muddy Waters.

4. An advertisement for the Mississippi Delta master Charlie Patton emphasizes the rural appeal of his style.

In general, later historians have concentrated on the rural Delta, but in terms of the 1920s recording boom, the most productive group of players in that region were based in W. C. Handy's old stomping grounds: the Beale Street entertainment district in Memphis. Like Atlanta, Memphis attracted versatile musicians who could please all the different people walking down a city street. Older players like Frank Stokes and Jim Jackson performed a similar range of material to what Willie McTell was playing in Atlanta, and their blues work included both rural-flavored styles and Handy's hits. Jackson is not much appreciated today, since his guitar work was relatively rudimentary, but he had one of the biggest hits of the era with 1927's "Kansas City Blues," which was imitated by dozens of other singers.

Memphis was also home to the era's two most successful jug bands, Cannon's Jug Stompers and the Memphis Jug Band. Such groups were common throughout the South, using cheap or homemade instruments to duplicate the sound of a more formal group: harmonicas and kazoos for clarinets, trumpets, and trombones; a jug for the tuba; a washtub, broomstick, and length of clothesline for a bass; and a washboard scraped with spoons or thimbles for percussion. Some of these bands were just kids playing for fun, but others were made up of polished, professional entertainers who used their odd instruments for novelty appeal, and their records did well enough that some New York and Chicago jazz artists pulled together jug and washboard groups to capitalize on the trend. The first jug band to hit on record was led by a violinist named Clifford Hayes in Louisville, Kentucky, but the Memphis bands made the most enduring impact thanks to their well-selected material and infectiously rowdy arrangements. Both groups were made up of expert, well-rehearsed performers—Cannon's harmonica player, Noah Lewis, was one of the great early masters of that instrument in blues—and along with being a lot of fun, they preserved a wealth of local music that might otherwise have been forgotten.

Urban blues

Historians treasure the variety and individuality of the country-identified blues players, but for the record companies the fad for rural-sounding artists had some clear disadvantages. Regional styles tend by definition to be more popular in some regions than others, and it is hard to build a consistent customer base by selling a disparate hodgepodge of idiosyncratic individualists. Pop music thrives on broad trends and reliable formulas, and it was much easier to come up with new blues queens than with new Lemon

Jeffersons—indeed, none of the other country artists equaled Jefferson's success. Most of the rural and street-corner artists also had only limited repertoires of blues, and when asked to come up with new material they did not tend to compose full songs: Most would just combine some old verses rather than write a cohesive lyric that was likely to be remembered and demanded by record buyers—or that could be successfully published as sheet music, which was still a major force in the music business. Furthermore, the record labels were based around New York and Chicago and preferred to work with professional performers who were available when needed and could perform whatever material was handed to them.

Such concerns took on added weight after the stock market crashed in September 1929, bringing on the Depression. Every sector of the music business was affected, and the record companies were particularly hard hit. They were already facing stiff competition from radio, which had better sound reproduction and broadcast the latest hits free of charge. Race records seem to have been relatively less threatened by radio than mainstream pop was, since in those racially segregated times African American performers rarely appeared on the airwaves. (Also, many people in areas like the Mississippi Delta were still living without electricity, so hand-cranked record players were the only music machines they could use.) Still, the new economic strictures put an end to the southern recording trips that had fed the country blues boom, and in any case the blues market was changing.

In the fall of 1928 the Vocalion label had released a pair of hits that would define a new wave of urban blues. The first was by a pianist and singer named Leroy Carr, who had been born in Nashville but raised in Indianapolis. Unlike either the vaudeville stars or the street singers, whose livelihood in that pre-microphone era had depended on having powerful voices, Carr sang as if he were sitting right next to the listener. It was the blues equivalent of Bing Crosby's pop crooning, and his intimate, romantic appeal was perfectly suited to records.

Carr's first hit, "How Long—How Long Blues," was a mournful lyric of longing for a departed lover, with his understated piano providing the rhythm and Scrapper Blackwell's guitar adding tasteful instrumental fills. The song was reworked from an old Ida Cox hit, but Carr soon established himself as a master songwriter, composing such enduring standards as "Midnight Hour Blues," "Blues Before Sunrise," and his masterpiece, "When the Sun Goes Down." As the titles suggest, these were wistful, late-night meditations, and the combination of evocative poetry and Carr's soulfully sincere delivery made him the most influential blues stylist for the next thirty years. Generations of singers would build on his model, from his contemporaries Bill Gaither (who billed himself as "Leroy's Buddy") and Bumble Bee Slim to the defining blues balladeers of the 1940s, T-Bone Walker and Charles Brown, mainstream performers like the Ink Spots and Nat King Cole, and eventually Ray Charles and Sam Cooke.

Two months after "How Long" appeared, a piano-guitar duo billed as Tampa Red and Georgia Tom released "It's Tight Like That," an upbeat party blues that was almost equally influential. Like Carr's hit, it had earlier roots, recycling the basic framework of Papa Charlie Jackson's "Shake that Thing," and it likewise inspired a flood of imitators—both blues specialists and mainstream bands and singers—spawning a rowdy, frequently risqué style recalled as "hokum." (Tampa Red was also an extremely influential slide guitar player, while Georgia Tom had been Ma Rainey's bandleader and—as Thomas A. Dorsey—would go on to be the father of modern gospel music and mentor to Mahalia Jackson.)

If the guitar was the perfect country blues instrument, the piano was particularly suited to the needs of black urbanites. Especially during Prohibition (1920–33), much of black nightlife was restricted to apartment "rent parties" or "buffet flats," which served as impromptu speakeasies and did not want a loud band that would disturb the neighbors or attract the law. In a small room, an intimate singer with a piano who could perform everything from pop ballads to low-down blues was the ideal musical entertainment. When Prohibition ended, saloons rushed to buy the newly popular jukeboxes—industry estimates suggest that up to half of all the records sold in the United States in the later 1930s went into commercial music machines—and the early electric speakers were particularly suited to the percussive power of a piano.

There had also been a significant shift in African American society. In 1900, 90 percent of African Americans still lived in the South, mostly in rural areas, but the early blues era overlapped a mass exodus to the urban north. By 1940 the proportion of blacks in the South had dropped to 77 percent, while in the same period the black population of Chicago rose from less than 2 percent of the city's total to more than 8 percent; the black population of Detroit rose from 1.4 percent to 9.2 percent; and the black population of Manhattan rose from 2 percent to almost 16 percent. Singers like Carr and Tampa Red had a cool, urbane hipness that fit well with city life and made both the blues queens and the country bluesmen sound old-fashioned by comparison. Roosevelt Sykes, a pianist and singer who was born in Arkansas and cut his musical teeth playing in the levee and lumber camps along the Mississippi River, moved on to St. Louis and Chicago as his recording career took off in the late 1920s. Soon he was singing about urban gambling dens and tossing off phrases like "Hello, Morning Glory, what's your story?"

The uptown flavor sold records not only to streetwise urbanites, but also to young rural southerners who wanted to sound like streetwise urbanites—Son House recalled that Robert Johnson routinely used terms like "Daddy-o." They also attracted fans who dismissed earlier blues styles as out of date: "It's Tight Like That" was a contemporary hip phrase—a term of approbation, with obvious reference to female genitalia—and the song was quickly issued on sheet music and covered by dance orchestras like Jimmie Noone's Apex Jazz Band, as well as spawning a flood of imitations and answer songs including Lonnie Johnson's "It Feels So Good," Charlie McCoy's "It Ain't No Good," and the Famous Hokum Boys' "It's All Used Up."

5. Lonnie Johnson recorded one of the many follow-ups to "It's Tight Like That," featuring a lyric spiced with both erotica and African exotica: "Monkey and the baboon playing in the grass / The baboon said no, but the monkey said yes."

Groups like the Hokum Boys also signaled a new pattern in blues recording. Rather than being a regular, working band, the Hokum Boys was just a name used by various studio groupings, at times including Tampa Red, Georgia Tom, Blind Blake, and Big Bill Broonzy. The success of the hokum-style groups reflected not only shifting fashions and recording trends, but also a new role for blues. In the early 1920s, the blues queens had been at the top of the black entertainment business, headlining shows that featured full orchestras, dancers, and comedians. By the late 1920s, though, African American performers were having more success with other styles of music: Ethel Waters was singing Tin Pan Alley pop hits like "Dinah" and "Sweet Georgia Brown," and appearing in Broadway shows and Hollywood movies. Louis Armstrong had evolved from a spectacular trumpeter who worked as an unbilled sideman for blues queens into a growling, laughing vocalist, popular with black and white listeners alike. Duke Ellington was becoming known as an innovative composer and bandleader, and Cab Calloway was singing his "hi-de-ho" songs for white Manhattanites and anyone who owned a radio. By 1936, a multiweek run by Bessie Smith at a New York nightclub was greeted by the *Chicago Defender* with the comment that she was "still tops...[but] the type of songs she featured have gone out of style."

Blues had not disappeared by any means, but it was now becoming associated with a particular audience. The word "jukebox" was derived from "juke" or "jook," southern slang for a rowdy, working-class drinking joint. The music-machine industry resisted the term for a decade, thinking it would give their product a bad reputation. But in the 1930s, musicians who had learned their trade in rural jukes, at urban rent parties, and in the lumber and levee camps along the Mississippi were finding ready customers across the country. The most popular included Roosevelt Sykes, Peetie Wheatstraw, and Walter Davis, and their music ranged from Carr-style ballads to upbeat, double-entendre hokum and the pounding rhythm called boogie-woogie.

The basic boogie style relied on heavy, repetitive bass-note patterns, typically played in the eight-beats-to-a-bar rhythm that would evolve into rock 'n' roll. This style seems to have been popular among black southern pianists by the turn of the century, and hit the national scene in 1929 with Pine Top Smith's "Pine Top's Boogie Woogie," a rollicking dance record spiced with spoken instructions: "I want everybody to dance 'em just like I tell you. And when I say 'Hold yourself,' I want all of you to get ready to stop. When I say, 'Stop,' don't move. And when I say 'Get it,' I want all of you-all to do a boogie-woogie." Hundreds of pianists over the next decades would work up their own versions of Smith's hit, and it may have transferred the name "boogie-woogie" from a dance to the piano style. Smith had challengers as the style's originator: Cow Cow Davenport, whose "Cow Cow Blues" had been a hit in 1928, printed up business cards that described him as "The man that gave America boogie-woogie." Whoever started the craze, its driving rhythm made it an ideal sound track for noisy bars, whether beaten out on an upright piano or blaring from a jukebox.

Meanwhile, the flood of hokum songs established blues as the favored medium for another kind of barroom entertainment: low-down, comic smut. There had always been dirty blues, but in the 1930s "party" records took on a new prominence—in part because they faced no competition from the heavily censored radio fare. In 1929 an albino pianist named Rufus Perryman, who worked under the name of Speckled Red, hit with a song inspired by an African American insult game, which he called "The Dirty Dozen." Songs based on "the dozens" had been around at least since the turn of the century, and seem to have been known throughout the country in extravagantly obscene versions—no rap lyric has gone farther in that direction—before Red cleaned one up for the record market. He matched his lyrics to a distinctive piano riff of descending, high-note triplets, and the record was so popular that within a year it inspired a raft of covers and sequels. Its success proved the appeal of raunchy blues that skirted the edge of acceptable language, and incidentally provided a brief heyday to a couple of rural blues artists: Blind Boy Fuller in North Carolina and Bo Carter in Mississippi both played the sort of guitar-based blues that had generally fallen out of fashion, but made up for their archaic sound with double-entendre themes like Fuller's "Let Me Squeeze Your Lemon" and "What Is That Smells Like Fish," and Carter's "Pussy Cat Blues" and "Banana in the Fruit Basket."

Fuller and Carter aside, the dominant blues sound of the 1930s was shaped in Chicago and St. Louis, where adept studio performers churned out hundreds of records with piano generally carrying the rhythm, guitar supplying high lead riffs, and sometimes a wailing harmonica or scraping washboard. More than any previous group of blues artists, these studio pros stuck to the regular twelve- and eight-bar forms, and they often played on one another's sessions, creating a uniform style that to modern listeners often seems repetitive. But to the record marketers it had the advantage of being consistent. Blues buyers cared less about novel instrumental approaches than about soulful vocals and distinctive lyrics. Peetie Wheatstraw, who billed himself as "The Devil's Son-in-Law," was known for his dark, moody voice and half-yodeled "ooh-well-well" interpolations (which were imitated by Robert Johnson, among others). Memphis Minnie, a terrific instrumentalist who was sometimes advertised as "the woman who plays guitar like a man," hit on record with double-entendre numbers like "Bumble Bee Blues" and "Me and My Chauffeur." Sonny Boy Williamson, remembered as the first great Chicago-based harmonica star, was known for party songs like "Good Morning, Little Schoolgirl" and a romping cover of Carr's "Sloppy Drunk Blues." Kokomo Arnold, a breathtakingly fast and eccentric slide guitarist, was known for the swooping falsetto whoop that made his "Milk Cow Blues" one of the most widely covered blues songs of the era by black and white singers alike.

The new urban blues style was almost as popular in white honky-tonks as in black juke joints. In 1939, a jukebox operator working

Prewar blues

45

for the Texas Novelty Company in Beaumont wrote to *Billboard* magazine that "Race records go good down in this South Texas city and surrounding territory. When we get a Race number that proves a hit we just leave it on the machine until it wears out. They don't get old and lose play like other records." All the artists he listed as favorites were midwestern studio regulars, and those tastes were echoed in numerous covers by white honky-tonk and western swing performers. Where once it had evoked images of elegantly gowned vaudeville queens or rough street corner shouters, blues was now America's late-night, barroom party music.

Chapter 3
Modern blues

Historians have tended to divide blues into prewar and postwar styles, in part due to the arrival of the electric guitar but also because the field has been dominated by record collectors, who find a natural break in the American Federation of Musicians' recording strike of 1942–44, during which no commercial records were made. The early 1940s was certainly a period of intense musical change in the United States, but all musical shifts are balanced by connections and continuities, and any attempt to categorize shifting blues styles is further complicated because the meaning of the word itself has kept changing. Today, we tend to think of blues as a genre, and to identify certain artists and bands with the style, but virtually no group chose to advertise itself as a blues band until the later 1940s and the billing did not become common until the 1960s. Some performers specialized in blues, particularly on records, but as long as popular music was based on live performances, no band wanted to be thought of as limited to a single kind of song.

One result is that many of the most popular and influential blues hits were by people we do not think of primarily as blues artists. In the mid-1930s, America was swept by the rhythm-centered style called "swing," which blended the orchestral arrangements of earlier dance orchestras with the blues-related harmonies and improvisations of New Orleans jazz. Some swing bands played more blues than others, but all demanded blues-influenced phrasing from their soloists. Benny Goodman got one of his biggest hits with a cover of Joe McCoy's twelve-bar lament "Why Don't You Do Right?" The Count Basie Orchestra, which many jazz historians consider the hardest-swinging band of all time, got its first big hit in 1937 with "One O'Clock Jump," a textbook exploration of the twelve-bar pattern, and remained focused on blues throughout its heyday.

Indeed, the rise of Basie and the other midwestern "territory bands" that shared his style makes it impossible to draw lines between jazz and blues in the later 1930s and '40s. Swing groups produced virtually all the biggest blues hits of the 1930s, and while some of those hits were instrumentals, many of the period's most important blues singers worked primarily as band vocalists. Jimmy Rushing, the male singer with the Basie orchestra, was a fine pop ballad singer but became so associated with twelve-bar hits like "Going to Chicago Blues" that eventually Basie would not let him sing anything else. The band's Tin Pan Alley numbers were performed by its female singer, Helen Humes—who, as it happens, had begun her recording career as a teenage blues queen in the 1920s, accompanied by Lonnie Johnson.

Another important singer who worked with Basie, Billie Holiday, named Bessie Smith as her main vocal influence and had her first success on record with the twelve-bar "Billie's Blues." The *Chicago Defender* described her in 1939 as being "looked upon by the public as one of the few remaining 'queens' of the blues," and her light-voiced, impeccably swinging variation of the classic style sparked a minor revival of female blues artists and made her the main model for Dinah Washington and generations of later singers.

In the 1930s, the combination of singers and dance orchestras was still a novelty. Before amplification and records became an important part of the music business, very few vocalists could make themselves heard over a brass-heavy orchestra, and in any case dance bands were playing for dancers, not listeners. Records, radio, and jukeboxes brought the two together: People hearing music at home or in a bar enjoyed having some vocals interspersed with the dance rhythms, and amplification made it possible for even the most delicate crooner to fit into a big band arrangement.

Amplification also brought other changes. At first, singers tended to be the only people using microphones on live gigs, but by the 1940s some small bands were beginning to be amplified as well, making them loud enough to work large ballroom dates. Jukeboxes and radio had already allowed small groups like Fats Waller's to rival the orchestras in popularity, and such combos became more important when the United States entered World War II, creating a drastic shortage of manpower in the music industry, as in other trades.

These shifts brought swing and blues even closer together. Big Bill Broonzy and Memphis Minnie recorded with horns, Basie cut small-group sessions featuring Leroy Carr songs, and innumerable singers and players blended down-home blues roots with swing inflections. Two of the most influential artists in this overlap were Dinah Washington and Louis Jordan. Washington, born Ruth Jones, started out singing gospel in Chicago, then switched to secular music and became the female vocalist for Lionel Hampton's big band. She established herself in 1944 with the double-sided hit of "Salty Papa Blues" and "Evil Gal Blues," the latter combining boasts about her evil disposition with a timely complaint about losing her man to Uncle Sam. An early review in the *Chicago Defender* suggests the way such material was viewed by the more sophisticated swing fans, calling Washington "a low-down blues warbler" and lamenting that "she was 'typing' Hampton's orchestra as an ordinary jukebox band."

Of course, "ordinary" can just be an elitist way of saying "popular." Hampton's band played a good deal besides blues, but in 1945 Washington's vocals helped him to win out over Basie and Duke Ellington in a *Defender* readers' poll, and he continued to hit with blues-oriented dance numbers into the rock 'n' roll era. Washington meanwhile went solo, and she quickly became America's dominant female blues stylist. She had the assurance of the old queens, a swing vocalist's sense of rhythm and melodic improvisation, and a range that extended from moody ballads to raunchy jive. The fact that blues was typed as low-down barroom music made it vital for an ambitious artist to expand into other genres. Washington managed to hit with mainstream pop and even country and western songs, and her versatility won her an exceptionally broad audience, filling venues that would have been dubious about booking someone known purely as a blues singer.

Blues was nonetheless a significant part of the pop mainstream in the early war years, and Holiday and Washington inspired a new wave of blues queens. When *Billboard* magazine began running a Race records chart in 1942, the biggest hit in its first year was Wee Bea Booze's revival of Ma Rainey's "See See Rider," and over the next decade Big Maybelle, Julia Lee, and Little Esther Phillips all reached broad audiences and helped shape the evolving R&B style.

Male blues artists were doing even better, perhaps because the music's association with a barroom atmosphere encouraged a masculine approach. Jimmy Rushing was joined by the big band shouters Wynonie Harris and Big Joe Turner, who belted out lyrics about booze and mean, mistreating mamas. In the 1940s, though, the most successful male blues star was an ebullient combo singer and alto saxophonist named Louis Jordan.

Jordan was originally from Arkansas, the son of a musician in the Rabbit's Foot Minstrels. He moved north in the 1930s and got a job with Chick Webb's orchestra at Harlem's Savoy Ballroom, and in 1938 he went solo, forming a hard-swinging band called the Tympany Five. (Tympani was misspelled, and the group tended to have more than five members, but he stuck with that name throughout his career.) Jordan was a hip musical comedian on the model of Louis Armstrong and Fats Waller, but after hitting in 1942 with Casey Bill Weldon's "I'm Gonna Leave You on the Outskirts of Town," he made blues a mainstay of his repertoire. In 1943 his wartime-themed "Ration Blues" crossed over to the pop charts, and for the next several years he was probably the most popular black entertainer in the United States, hitting with a series of twelve-bar blues and boogie-woogies including "Caldonia," "Choo-Choo Ch'Boogie," and "Let the Good Times Roll."

Jordan's style, which is remembered as "jump blues," was essentially a stripped-down version of the Basie approach, with powerhouse rhythms and shouted vocals. After he added Carl Hogan on electric guitar, his group set a pattern that would be imitated in the 1950s by Bill Haley, Chuck Berry, and hundreds of rock 'n' rollers. In the 1940s, though, horns and piano were still the dominant instruments, and Jordan's immediate followers were boogie-woogie combo leaders including Amos Milburn, Joe and Jimmy Liggins, and Memphis Slim. These small, amplified groups served notice that the days of the big dance orchestras were numbered, though many of the big bands also did their best to cash in on the blues and boogie-woogie trend: The top-selling blues hits of the 1940s included records by Basie, Earl Hines, Woody Herman, and Tommy Dorsey.

The West Coast sound

African Americans had been emigrating from the rural South to urban industrial centers in ever-increasing numbers since the Civil War, but until the 1940s most had headed for the cities of the East and Midwest. Though black communities in Los Angeles and the San Francisco Bay Area had grown steadily, they remained tiny compared to those in Chicago, St. Louis, and Harlem. The attack on Pearl Harbor in December 1941 changed that situation overnight, creating a desperate need for laborers in the West Coast's shipbuilding yards. Young men and women flooded in from Texas, Oklahoma, and Louisiana—all prime states for the older blues styles—almost tripling Los Angeles's black population and quintupling Oakland's. As a result, in the 1940s the West Coast became the center of blues innovation. Young, newly arrived black listeners wanted to hear sounds that had the grit and energy they were used to from back home but that were hipper than their parents' music. In some ways, it was like the situation that had spawned the unique Delta blues sound of the 1920s, but Los Angeles in particular was a major city and—thanks to Hollywood—an entertainment center that was beginning to rival New York. So, where Mississippi had produced the earthiest, most rhythm-focused style of blues, the West Coast blues was noted for its urbane sophistication.

This style is perfectly exemplified by Nat King Cole's first hit, a twelve-bar ballad from 1941 called "That Ain't Right." Cole's voice blended Leroy Carr's intimate feel with a smooth jazz lilt, framed by his sparkling piano and the supple electric guitar of Oscar Moore. His King Cole trio, which appeared regularly on radio and was marketed by the new Capitol label in its mainstream pop line, charmed everyone from young factory workers to Hollywood stars. Dozens of similar groups soon appeared, including the Three Blazers, led by Oscar Moore's brother Johnny and featuring a pianist and singer named Charles Brown. The Blazers were so coolly sophisticated that their first record was an instrumental titled "Fugue in C major," but their biggest hit was 1945's "Drifting Blues," which became an enduring standard thanks to Brown's mellow phrasing and the evocative opening lines: "I'm drifting and drifting, like a ship out on the sea." Other moody blues ballads followed, including the perennial "Merry Christmas Baby," and after leaving the group in 1949 Brown had a dozen hits on his own, including the phenomenally popular "Black Night," and a cover of Carr's "When the Sun Goes Down."

Brown and the Moore brothers had come to Los Angeles from Texas, and the West Coast scene in general was dominated by Texans and Oklahomans, including Ivory Joe Hunter, Eddie Vinson, Amos Milburn, Lowell Fulson, and T-Bone Walker. These performers ranged from smooth balladeers to upbeat honky-tonkers, but all blended a basic knowledge of swing with roots in the work of older bluesmen such as Carr and Lemon Jefferson. (Walker recalled meeting Jefferson as a child, and Fulson briefly accompanied Texas Alexander.) Their mix of southern roots and urban sophistication would shape the next generation's idea of blues, especially in the South. Along with their own records and touring, they inspired young followers like B. B. King, who was born in Mississippi and had his first hit in Memphis, but based his style overwhelmingly on the West Coasters.

As usual, the blues audience of the 1940s was more interested in vocals than in instrumental skills, but in hindsight one of the most important things about the West Coast performers was the new focus they placed on electric guitar. The defining figure in this context was Aaron "T-Bone" Walker, who first recorded in 1929 as a Leroy Carr clone and moved to Los Angeles in the mid-1930s. In 1943 he took over the guitar chair in an interracial combo led by the white boogie-woogie pianist Freddie Slack and recorded his first masterpiece, "Mean Old World." The vocals still had traces of Carr, with an overlay of Kansas City swing, but the guitar work was a startling innovation. Walker mixed the harmonic sensibility and precision of Oscar and Johnny Moore with a deep blues feel, the bite of the older slide players, and the energy of the bluesier saxophonists, blazing a trail that would be followed by virtually all the electric blues and rock guitar heroes to come. Indeed, one of his style's greatest strengths was its adaptability: Whether playing with Basie-style orchestras, Jordan-style jump combos, or, in the 1950s, with Chicago-style bar bands, Walker's guitar lines fitted perfectly. Few players ever captured the full scope of his musicianship, but thousands found something to borrow or imitate.

Walker was also a spectacular showman, moving with a dancer's grace and doing the splits while playing his guitar behind his head. Such acrobatics went back to Charlie Patton, Tommy Johnson, and the all-around instrumental entertainers in medicine shows and vaudeville. But it was Walker who matched

6. T-Bone Walker was a dynamic dancer and a suave blues balladeer, but he is best remembered as the defining virtuoso of electric lead guitar.

them with the new possibilities of the electric guitar, making him a model for everyone from southwestern bluesmen like Gatemouth Brown to Chuck Berry and eventually Jimi Hendrix.

The wave of artists inspired by Walker, Washington, and Jordan not only changed the sound of blues but revitalized the music's image, stripping it of its rural associations in favor of hip dance rhythms and Carr-like introspection. "This is a mean old world, baby, to live in by yourself," Walker sang, in a classic urban lament, and followed up with the most famous blues ballad of all time, "Call It Stormy Monday (But Tuesday Is Just as Bad)." The latter title was a link to the swing mainstream—Earl Hines and Billy Eckstine had hit with a previous "Stormy Monday Blues"—but Walker's electrified ballad became so popular that its model has been all but forgotten.

Rhythm and blues

By the late 1940s, the big bands that had dominated American popular music through the Depression years were falling on hard times, hit first by the wartime manpower shortage and then by the pressures of amplification, a widespread slump in the dance business, and skyrocketing postwar prices. Meanwhile, new technologies including light, unbreakable vinyl records (which made it easier for small record labels to get their product to retailers) and television (which became the main national broadcast medium, forcing radio to search out niche and local audiences) gave new prominence to previously ghettoized styles like Race and hillbilly music. In 1949 *Billboard* magazine adopted new names for its nonmainstream pop charts: "country and western" for the white southern style, and "rhythm and blues" for the African American market. Since the point of the rhythm and blues chart was to indicate black consumer tastes, it continued to include records by African American big bands and pop balladeers, but over the next few years the term "R&B" would also become increasingly associated with a particular style of music, exemplified by the stripped-down instrumentation and powerful beat of the jump blues combos.

Following Louis Jordan's model, many of the most distinctive instrumentalists in early R&B were saxophonists. In particular, the late 1940s brought a wave of tenor "honkers" who eschewed melodic improvisation in favor of minimalist rhythmic punch. The honking style was established by Illinois Jaquet's one-note solo on Lionel Hampton's 1942 record of "Flying Home," but reached its apogee on records such as Big Jay McNeely's twelve-bar instrumental, "The Deacon's Hop," a number one hit of 1949. McNeely played one or two notes over and over, in a sexy growl that gradually rose to a series of wild honks and screams, and his approach was shared by Joe Houston, Willis "Gator Tail" Jackson, and many others.

Between singers and honkers, five of the twelve records that topped *Billboard*'s rhythm and blues chart in 1949 were straight twelve-bar blues, and the other seven included Jimmy Witherspoon's reworking of Alberta Hunter's "Ain't Nobody's Business," Charles Brown reviving a Carr-style eight-bar ballad called "Trouble Blues" (which traced back to the Tennessee country bluesman Sleepy John Estes), two Louis Jordan numbers, a rocking boogie by Wynonie Harris, and a spare, acoustic-guitar-backed shuffle called "Boogie Chillen'" by the Mississippi-born guitarist John Lee Hooker. In 1950 the numbers were even more striking: twelve-bar blues accounted for eight of the first ten records to top the chart, all but one of which came from Los Angeles. It was the high point for straight-ahead blues on the national scene, and the success of the West Coast sound spawned offshoots across the country.

One particularly fertile area was New Orleans, which had been closely connected to California for many decades, thanks to busy shipping routes and a direct New Orleans–Los Angeles railroad line. Now, local blues artists combined the West Coast style with the city's Caribbean-flavored rhythms. The standard-bearer of this fusion was a young pianist and singer named Antoine "Fats" Domino, who made his debut in 1949 with an eight-bar blues called "The Fat Man." It was based on "Junker's Blues," a piano-driven saga of drug users and petty criminals recorded ten years earlier by Champion Jack Dupree, which Domino rewrote as a light-hearted party anthem, setting off a string of hits that made him the most popular R&B performer of the 1950s.

The New Orleans rhythmic fusion resulting in twelve-bar rumbas and mambos as well as straightforward boogie-woogie, and if Domino was its most visible practitioner, its grand master was an eccentric keyboard wizard named Roy Byrd, who billed himself as Professor Longhair. Byrd had only one national hit, 1950's "Bald Head," but his intricately danceable rhythms, oddball humor, and quirky vocals made him a local favorite. Of his many twelve-bar compositions, "Mardi Gras In New Orleans" became an annual carnival standard, while "Tipitina," a mess of Creole patois, nonsense syllables, and yodeling, remains the crowning testament to his weird brilliance. Longhair's colorful compatriots included Huey "Piano" Smith and the Clowns—famed for "Rocking Pneumonia and the Boogie-Woogie Flu"—Eddie Bo, and Sugar Boy Crawford, all of whom explored a mix of rumba, blues, and off-the-wall lyrics.

New Orleans remained a unique musical melting pot, but the diaspora of African Americans from the rural south to cities throughout the United States, and the growing prominence of records, were blurring most regional boundaries. In Memphis, a piano player named Rosco Gordon matched the New Orleans approach with 1952's "No More Doggin'"—a loping blues, which, thanks to the power of radio to cross international boundaries, became the foundation of Jamaican ska. The Memphis scene got an added boost in the early 1950s when an entrepreneur named Sam Phillips opened a recording studio where out-of-town producers could cut local talent, then founded his own label, Sun Records. The war years had seen an explosion of such small companies, and with the major labels concentrating on mainstream pop, they became the dominant force in the country and R&B markets.

The major blues figures who made their recording debuts in Phillips's studio included Gordon, Howlin' Wolf, Ike Turner, and Little Milton—and later the rockabilly singers Elvis Presley, Carl Perkins, and Jerry Lee Lewis—but in terms of later blues trends, the most important Memphian to emerge in this period was Riley "B. B." King. Born in Indianola, Mississippi, King worked as a deejay on Memphis's WDIA, "The Mother Station of the Negroes," where he acquired his trademark initials as the "Beale Street Blues Boy," and he was keenly aware of the latest R&B fashions. His guitar work showed an obvious debt to Walker and the other West Coasters—with the addition of a stinging vibrato inspired by the slide playing of his cousin Booker White and an improvisational grace he traced to the Belgian Gypsy guitarist Django Reinhardt—but what made him a star were his passionate, church-inflected vocals. Bringing the innovations of gospel quartet leads such as Sam McCrary of the Fairfield Four and Ira Tucker of the Dixie Hummingbirds into the blues world, King not only reshaped blues but also helped lay the foundation of the soul revolution.

As with Blind Willie Johnson's work, this was part of an ongoing process: The quartet leads, along with female stars like Mahalia Jackson, had revolutionized African American religious music in the 1940s by adapting blues techniques, then adding a Pentecostal fervor that inspired their audiences with religious ecstasy. They stretched their vocal phrases with intricate melisma—the practice of taking a single syllable and carrying it over a series of notes—and spiced them with growls, shouts, and screams. Both Dinah Washington and Lowell Fulson had made some use of these techniques, and Ray Charles would carry them wholesale into the R&B world, becoming known as the father of soul. But at the beginning of the 1950s, King was the main trailblazer in defining a modern blues approach that drew on the oldest traditions of the African American South.

The Chicago style

Though the sophisticated urban swing of the West Coast artists was the best-selling blues style of the postwar period, some fans continued to prefer the rawer "down home" sounds of the rural South. Especially in the industrial centers of the Midwest, an older generation of black migrants had not forgotten the music of their youth, and during the war years they had been joined by a new wave of folks from back home. Mississippi lost almost a tenth of its African American population during the 1940s, with Chicago the most popular destination. One of those migrants, McKinley "Muddy Waters" Morganfield, left Stovall's Plantation outside Clarksdale for Chicago in 1943, drawn by the wartime boom in factory jobs, and he soon got together with other Mississippi musicians and began playing at rent parties and neighborhood bars.

At Delta picnics, Waters had played a mix of pop songs, country and western, and contemporary blues hits, but compared to the West Coast artists his sound was clearly archaic. When he tried to work some gigs with his cousin Eddie Boyd, one of Chicago's reigning blues combo leaders, he lost the job because he could not mimic Johnny Moore's smooth guitar leads. Nonetheless, for a lot of transplanted Mississippians his electrified version of the Delta style was a perfect combination of old and new. His vocals mixed field hollers and moans with touches of wry humor, and his slide guitar lines put electric overdrive on licks learned from Son House and Robert Johnson.

Johnson, who had died in 1938, is often grouped with House's generation of prewar Mississippi artists, but he had been born in 1911, only two years before Waters. As a young innovator, he had inspired his Delta peers by breaking into the record business and creating a body of work that summed up the local tradition and blended it with the hip sounds of urban stars like Carr, Kokomo Arnold, and Lonnie Johnson. At first this fusion received little attention outside the Delta, but it became a basic building block of the later Chicago sound—a connection made explicit by Johnson's stepson and protégé, Robert Lockwood, who established himself as one of the city's most influential guitarists.

By chance, Johnson's records also led to Waters's first recordings by inspiring Alan Lomax to bring a team of folklorists to the Delta in 1941 in search of similar artists. Lomax and the Fisk University professor John W. Work recorded Waters at his home on Stovall's Plantation, and Waters later recalled that the experience of hearing himself on these records was what convinced him he could be a serious professional. Waters's early Chicago hits included electric versions of the same songs he played on those field recordings, giving later listeners a rare glimpse of exactly how he reshaped his country style to fit a new world.

Those first hits came in the late 1940s, after Waters met Leonard Chess, one of the owners of a small label called Aristocrat Records. (In 1950, after Chess and his brother Phil bought out their partners, it was renamed Chess Records.) Chess owned a popular jazz and blues club, and Waters's music at first struck him as too primitive to be marketable, but he was persuaded to give it a shot, and the result helped to set off a new wave of down-home blues. Along with Detroit's John Lee Hooker, Waters electrified the rural Delta style without losing either its raw power or its complex rhythmic and tonal inflections. Although some listeners found his style *too* raw—he regularly appeared on the R&B charts through the 1950s but never got a number one hit—to many people it epitomizes the greatest strengths of the blues idiom. Indeed, as Robert Palmer pointed out in *Deep Blues*, the defining study of the Delta-Chicago style, the apparent rawness of Waters's work was deceptive:

His mastery of the fine points of intonation is the true glory of his singing. Those infinitesimally flattened thirds, majestic falling fifths, and glancing slides between tones all *mean* something, just as the slightest shift in the pitch level of a person's speech means something....A musician trained in, say, the classical music of India, which puts a premium on the ability to hear and execute fine microtonal shadings, would recognize in the astonishing precision and emotional richness...something very close to his own tradition.

Waters did not describe his music in these terms, but he was acutely conscious of having skills that younger, city-bred musicians lacked. Like Hooker, who hewed even closer to the free, unrhymed approach of the old hollers, he regarded himself as one of the last bearers of a great and vanishing tradition. At the same time, he was proud of the ways he had modernized the older sounds. Where T-Bone Walker used electric sustain to mimic jazz horn lines, Waters used it to strip his playing down to essentials, filling the space between notes with ominous power. On his breakthrough record, 1948's "I Can't Be Satisfied," his slide lines had a ferocious whine that could cut through a noisy urban bar, while his interplay with Big Crawford's stand-up bass displayed the intricate polyrhythms that had always been a Delta specialty.

That stripped-down sound sold well in Chicago, but after a while Waters decided he was ready for something else and persuaded Chess to record the band he had been working with on live gigs. This group included Little Walter, a Louisiana-born harmonica player with whom Waters shared an almost psychic musical bond. Their second record, "Louisiana Blues," made the national R&B top ten, and with its heavy, booming sound and a line about "going down in New Orleans [to] get me a mojo hand," it forged an image of Waters as a dark Delta hoodoo man. Over the next few years he cut a string of slow, earthy hits whose moaning harmonica and gritty slide guitar were the antithesis of the West Coast style. But if Waters's music sounded old-fashioned to some fans, Leonard Chess's son Marshall recalled to the R&B historian

Arnold Shaw that it hit the local crowds like Elvis Presley hit the rock 'n' roll scene: "It was sex. If you had ever seen Muddy then, the effect he had on the women! Because blues has always been a women's market. On Saturday night they'd line up ten deep."

By the early 1950s, Waters's mix of electricity and rural roots was being exploited by a generation of southern players, including Lightnin' Hopkins in Houston; Elmore James in Jackson, Mississippi; Sonny Boy Williamson in Helena, Arkansas; and Chester "Howlin' Wolf" Burnett in Memphis. Some of these artists went north—Howlin' Wolf moved to Chicago in 1952, and James followed the next year after hitting with a reworking of Robert Johnson's "I Believe I'll Dust My Broom"—but others stuck to their home bases. Hopkins never felt comfortable outside of Houston, and though Williamson became a Chess stalwart, touring the United States and Europe, he regularly returned to his radio gig as a musician and pitchman for King Biscuit flour in Helena. (This Sonny Boy Williamson, who was originally named Aleck Miller, is a different person from the John Lee "Sonny Boy" Williamson who was the defining Chicago blues harmonica master of the 1930s and '40s—though, a bit confusingly, he was older than the earlier recording artist.)

Howlin' Wolf was the most ferociously charismatic of the electric down-home stars. He recorded a double-sided hit for Chess in 1951 while still in Memphis, moved north the next year, and became Waters's main rival on the Chicago scene. Both he and Williamson claimed that they had been playing electrified Delta blues before Waters did, and there is no reason to disbelieve them—records were not the whole story, and Williamson in particular had become a radio star in the Delta region on *King Biscuit Time*, which featured him with a backing band that included Robert Lockwood. Similarly, Wolf had a radio show in Memphis and was recording for both Chess and the rival RPM label; he later boasted that he arrived in Chicago with "a four-thousand-dollar car and $3,900 in my pocket. I'm the onliest one

7. The Texas guitarist and singer Lightnin' Hopkins put four records in the R&B top ten but continued to do most of his work in small venues like this Houston juke joint.

drove out of the South like a gentleman." Such comments are a reminder that devotion to rural or archaic styles did not mean lack of interest in commercial success. Wolf was an astute businessman and bandleader, and although his 1956 hit "Smokestack Lightnin'" could accurately be characterized as an old-fashioned, one-chord field holler, it was also a brilliantly arranged R&B single, performed with impeccable precision and stage-grabbing showmanship.

Many fans and scholars continue to hail the work of Wolf, Waters, and their peers as a high point of the blues genre, but by the mid-1950s musical fashions were changing yet again. It is no accident that the biggest hit to come out of the Chicago down-home scene featured Little Walter, who was 17 years younger than Waters and twenty years younger than Wolf. Walter was a fine interpreter of the older Mississippi styles, but he was also an innovator who had modeled his harmonica style on Louis Jordan's saxophone riffs. His defining instrumental hit, "Juke," recorded in 1952 while he was still with Waters's band, topped the R&B chart for two months, and his records continued to outsell Waters's and Wolf's, though the older men retained a solid audience for their live performances. Waters also updated his sound somewhat, thanks to Willie Dixon, the Chess label's house bass player, chief producer, and songwriter. Dixon wrote a funny, boastful number called "I'm Your Hoochie Coochie Man" that built on Waters's "mojo" image, and it became Waters's biggest hit with its trademark "duh-duh-duh, duh-duh" riff being copied by younger R&B stars including Ray Charles, Ruth Brown, the Robins (later known as the Coasters), and a hillbilly-flavored St. Louis singer and guitarist named Chuck Berry.

Those younger artists were all part of a shift in which "rhythm and blues" was evolving from an updated euphemism for "Race" into a modern pop style. By the mid-1950s, white teenagers were tuning in to R&B radio stations, and a Cleveland disc jockey named Alan Freed popularized a new term for the music that avoided any lingering racial connotations: rock 'n' roll. In 1955 Berry went to Chess Records on Waters's recommendation and cut "Maybellene," which not only became a major R&B hit but crossed over to the pop charts. The next year RCA signed Elvis Presley, who had already attracted attention with a handful of blues-oriented singles on the Sun label. By the second half of the 1950s, radios and record players around the world were blaring the music of a generation of young rock 'n' rollers—not only black and white Americans but Latin Americans, Europeans, Asians, and local stars in countries as disparate as Egypt and Australia. Blues was reaching a wider audience than ever before—but most people were no longer calling it blues.

Rock 'n' roll arrives

As with the line between blues and jazz, the line between blues and rock 'n' roll is a matter of opinion and taxonomy. The basic twelve-bar blues form was recycled ad infinitum for rock 'n' roll hits, from Berry's "Johnny B. Goode" to Little Richard's "Tutti Frutti," Bill Haley's "Rock Around the Clock," Buddy Holly's "Peggy Sue," and the soon-to-be-ubiquitous "Twist." Waters's "Hoochie Coochie Man" provided a slight variation, doubling the first four bars of the standard progression to create a sixteen-bar blues, and that model was followed in Carl Perkins's "Blue Suede Shoes" and Presley's "Jailhouse Rock."

Whether one wants to call all of those songs blues is a matter of choice, but two things are clear: by a strict chordal definition they were blues, and yet the arrival of rock 'n' roll hurt a lot of blues-identified performers. From Louis Jordan and T-Bone Walker to Muddy Waters and Howlin' Wolf, the focus on teen-oriented, good-time dance music threatened older artists, and especially those whose music addressed adult themes and concerns. In 1957, as Berry was singing a perky twelve-bar lyric aimed directly at the kids—"Up in the morning and out to school / The teacher is teaching the golden rule"—Muddy Waters was recording "Got My Mojo Working," another tribute to African-derived magical traditions. Sonny Boy Williamson was singing about hard-won knowledge: "It took me a long time to find out my mistake / But I bet you my bottom dollar, I'm not fattening no more frogs for snakes." B. B. King was celebrating his "Sweet Little Angel" in thoroughly adult terms: "When she spreads her wings around me, I get joy and everything." Soon Bobby "Blue" Bland, King's one-time chauffeur, would get his first hit with a worldly-wise warning: "Further on up the road, someone's gonna hurt you like you hurt me."

There was still an audience for older blues styles: all these records sold decently, although the Waters and Williamson entries did not do well enough to make the national charts. But the teenagers of the 1950s wanted to hear their own music. Most African American city kids felt little connection to the rural South—nor, in the midst of the blossoming civil rights movement, did they want to.

By the early 1960s the musicians who remained devoted to blues were either getting day jobs, relying on a shrinking audience of older listeners, or trying to find ways to modernize their sound. Meanwhile, the artists whose skills encompassed more than blues were exploring other directions: Dinah Washington crossed over to the pop charts with string-laden ballads and slick soul duets. Ray Charles forged a new style by grafting sexy lyrics onto gospel songs, then branched out into pop and country and western.

B. B. King worked both sides of the line, cutting pop-style records with lush arrangements and back-up choruses while continuing to play his older style on live dates and occasional breakthrough hits like 1960's "Sweet Sixteen." The gospel-inflected "soul" style was taking off, and if King's arrangements were somewhat old-fashioned, his vocals fit the new sound. He had also inspired a generation of younger performers in Memphis and Chicago, among them Albert King, Little Milton, Otis Rush, and Buddy Guy. Some of these artists stuck to basic blues styles on record, featuring electric guitar and harmonica, while others cut horn-powered soul discs. In either case, what got recorded did not necessarily bear much relation to what they played at gigs. Producers and label owners made most of the recording decisions, and artists who were playing soul hits in the clubs might be judged more effective as blues artists on disc, or vice versa. Guy was known on record for gritty blues with killer guitar lines and vocals ornamented with King's falsetto cry, but he recalled that in the Chicago bars "every joint we played in had a jukebox and if you couldn't play those Top 10 numbers on the jukebox, you wasn't gonna play in this club!" Muddy Waters continued to feature his old hits in his familiar style, but his band would fill out his shows with soul vocals and hard bop instrumentals.

As with rock 'n' roll, the line between blues and soul was often hard to draw—Ike and Tina Turner first hit the charts in 1960 with a twelve-bar blues, "A Fool in Love," and five years later

James Brown would herald the arrival of funk with a pair of twelve-bar workouts, "Papa's Got a Brand New Bag" and "I Got You (I Feel Good)." Etta James was Chess Record's dominant female star, and though all of her hits for the label were clearly in the soul bag, a 1964 live album found her mixing that sound with songs learned from Waters, B. B. King, and Jimmy Reed.

Meanwhile, in Louisiana, the Latin grooves that formed the rhythmic foundation of the soul-funk movement fit perfectly with New Orleans's Caribbean-inflected blues style. The pianist and producer Allen Toussaint and his studio band, which would evolve into the transcendently funky Meters, exemplified this style with 1966's "Get Out of My Life, Woman," a twelve-bar blues hit for the singer Lee Dorsey. Slim Harpo, a laid-back guitarist and harmonica player from south-central Louisiana, drew on a similar range of influences: his biggest hit, "Baby, Scratch My Back," was a sexy monologue over a hip rhythm riff that was routinely covered by soul bands.

A few artists continued to reach the national market with more down-home, old-fashioned styles. Jimmy Reed was a traditional-sounding bluesman, singing in a relaxed country drawl backed by his own whining harmonica and boogie shuffle guitar, but he hit consistently through the late 1950s and early 1960s and had his songs covered by young soul and rock 'n' roll stars.

By the 1960s, though, the term "blues" had largely fallen out of favor with black pop listeners. James Brown grew up with the music of Blind Boy Fuller and Tampa Red and had some of his biggest successes with the twelve-bar form, but in his autobiography he insisted that "I still don't like the blues. Never have." The soul era was a time of burgeoning black pride, and if life was hard in the ghettos of urban America, young African Americans still had no interest in being reminded of the southern cotton fields. So by the mid-1960s, the blues label was increasingly being limited to artists who were not seen as part of the contemporary pop scene, and especially older players who appealed to the growing folk and rock audiences.

The folk-blues revival

By the dawn of the 1960s, a new blues audience was appearing in coffeehouses, on college campuses, and in European concert halls. Jazz and folk scholars had been tangentially interested in blues since the 1920s, and a handful of artists—Huddie "Lead Belly" Ledbetter, Josh White, and Big Bill Broonzy—had found secondary careers playing for white, middle-class fans in New York cabarets, college folk-music clubs, and in Europe. In 1958, on Broonzy's recommendation, the English jazz trombonist Chris Barber arranged a tour with Muddy Waters, giving Britain a first taste of electric blues. (Some fans loved it, others complained about the volume.) And in the summer of 1960 Waters provided a similar surprise to American jazz fans when he brought his full band to the Newport Jazz Festival for an afternoon of blues that also included John Lee Hooker, Jimmy Rushing, the boogie-woogie pianist Sammy Price, and the rural Louisiana fiddle-and-guitar duo of Butch Cage and Willie Thomas. Two years later, a pair of German promoters put together a touring program they billed as "The American Folk-Blues Festival," bringing Hooker, T-Bone Walker, Memphis Slim, Helen Humes, and the acoustic duo of Brownie McGhee and Sonny Terry to Germany, France, and Great Britain, and they continued to host similar tours each year through 1969.

As those bills suggest, the folk and jazz promoters' approach to blues tended to be explicitly historical. Taking John Hammond's 1938 "From Spirituals to Swing" Carnegie Hall concert as a model, they created educational programs that traced the music's development from a rural style through its urban mutations and up to the electric sounds of the early 1950s. In keeping with that approach, they avoided anything that smacked of commercial showbiz: European promoters persuaded T-Bone Walker not

to dance or do the splits, and though Buddy Guy was filmed
jiving his way through a cover of James Brown's "Out of Sight"
at the beginning of the 1965 Folk-Blues Festival tour, he was
asked to avoid such material on future dates. The Newport Folk
Festival—an offshoot of the jazz event—was even more single-
mindedly focused on traditional styles. Hooker appeared there
in 1963, but with an acoustic guitar and no band, and that year's
other blues artists were McGhee and Terry, Mississippi John Hurt,
the Reverend Gary Davis, and two young, white acoustic guitarists
and singers, Dave Van Ronk and John Hammond.

With the exception of Hooker, who was still touring regionally on
the African American club circuit, the other blues artists featured
at Newport were working exclusively on the burgeoning folk
scene. The "folk revival" provided a welcome new audience for
some older artists and attracted young performers to the older
styles, but the folk aesthetic placed a premium on rural-sounding

8. The afternoon blues workshop at the 1963 Newport Folk Festival.
From *left*: John Hammond, Mississippi John Hurt, Clarence Cooper,
Dave Van Ronk, Sonny Terry, and John Lee Hooker.

styles, which meant that its blues component was usually limited to male singer-guitarists. The insistence on rural purity was sometimes taken to ridiculous extremes: When Sam Charters published the first book-length study of blues in 1959, with an accompanying album that included tracks by Blind Lemon Jefferson, Blind Willie McTell, Lonnie Johnson, and Leroy Carr, both were titled *The Country Blues*—and some hardcore fans were so incensed at the inclusion of urbanites like Johnson and Carr that they issued a rival LP titled *Really! The Country Blues*.

Though few fans insisted on that level of purity, the revivalists in general came to blues with different tastes and standards than previous audiences had. In the past, blues had attracted listeners with catchy dance rhythms, rowdy humor, and songs that reflected the fans' lives, troubles, and dreams. The revivalists, by contrast, were looking for an alternative to the light entertainment of the pop scene and for insight into vanished or foreign worlds. As a result, versatile professionals who had adapted their work to the popular market—Carr, Tampa Red, T-Bone Walker, Dinah Washington—were devalued in favor of performers who exemplified older-sounding, more obviously regional styles, and occasionally an introspective songwriter such as Skip James, who could be appreciated as a folk poet.

The revivalist aesthetic brought new attention to some wonderful artists, a few of whom were "rediscovered" and found new careers in the twilight of their lives. The most successful of these was a Delta guitarist and singer named Mississippi John Hurt. Hurt was a farmer and occasional bootlegger who played music primarily for his own amusement, and as a result he had not needed to keep up with commercial trends. His style and repertoire reached back to the nineteenth century and had already sounded old-fashioned when he made his first records in 1928. However, to folk audiences his mix of country dance tunes, ragtime ditties, badman ballads, religious songs, and early blues provided a variety that was lacking in the work of his more modern-sounding,

The Blues

blues-focused contemporaries. He was also an exceptionally charming performer, with a sparkling sense of humor to match his warm, gentle voice and crisp guitar work.

The folk-blues fans were trying not only to revive and preserve older styles but also to establish the music they loved as serious, valuable art. Along with recording and promoting rural performers, they interviewed them, researched their past, and attempted to analyze and classify regional and historical styles. Musicians like Hurt, who played relatively little blues, were dubbed "songsters" (a common synonym for "singer" in the rural South), and valued for the breadth of their repertoires and their preservation of pre-twentieth-century styles. Collectors sought out the records of Henry "Ragtime Texas" Thomas, who had recorded a uniquely varied and archaic repertoire in the late 1920s, and discovered previously unrecorded players such as the Texan Mance Lipscomb, who like Hurt had been born in the 1890s but made his first record for the collector-oriented Arhoolie label in 1960.

Along with presenting living artists, the revivalists organized reissues of old records. The early ventures were on specialist labels such as Folkways and Riverside, but in 1961 Columbia released an LP of Robert Johnson's recordings, titled *King of the Delta Blues Singers*. Since the late 1930s, a small clique of jazz and folk fans had regarded Johnson as an exceptional figure, and this album established him as a mysterious Mississippi genius whose work was the foundation not only of most later blues but—in the minds of some particularly devoted fans—of all rock 'n' roll. Johnson's formidable talent and broad command of the 1930s blues scene, from Delta slide to urban sophistication, made him a perfect choice to introduce new listeners to prewar styles, but where his peers had tended to admire him for up-to-date boogie shuffles like "Sweet Home Chicago" and "I Believe I'm Going to Dust My Broom," the Columbia album focused on the oldest and most eerily poetic songs in his repertoire: slide guitar pieces learned from Son House and haunting compositions such as "Hellhound on My Trail." His skilled songwriting, brilliant guitar work, and darkly moving vocals were supplemented with legends about how he had sold his soul to the devil at a rural crossroads and stories of how he had been killed by a jealous husband.

For many young fans, Johnson exemplified not only an ideal of blues music but also a romantic image of the blues life. And, since he was dead, these fans turned to the surviving artists who had a similar style or mystique. House was brought out of retirement and amazed college audiences with the trance-like passion of his performances. Booker (often spelled "Bukka") White and Robert Pete Williams recorded long, improvised songs that suggested the lyrical richness that had been missed by the three-minute limitation of the old 78s. And Skip James, whose "Devil Got My Woman" had been the model for Johnson's "Hellhound," was finally recognized as not a juke joint entertainer but a great artist.

James sang in a high, intense voice and played in an unusual, minor key style on both guitar and piano, and although he first recorded in 1931, he was barely known outside his home town of Bentonia, south of the Delta. More than any other major blues performer, James seems to have approached his music in the self-absorbed manner of a Western academic artist, sticking to his own aesthetic choices and making few concessions to his audiences' tastes. The emotional power of his work was lost on most blues fans in the 1930s, but it clearly appealed to Johnson, and the revivalists hailed it as the poetic testament of a unique genius.

By contrast, most revivalists had little or no interest in the blues-oriented stars of the R&B scene. When *Urban Blues*, the first book-length study of contemporary electric styles, appeared in 1966, the author Charles Keil estimated that about 70 percent of African American music listeners were interested in soul music (in which he included blues); out of that some 20 percent supported contemporary, blues-focused artists such as B. B. King,

Albert King, Freddy King, Bobby Bland, and Little Milton; and fewer than 10 percent had any interest in down-home players like Waters and Hooker. Meanwhile, some white jazz and folk fans had discovered Hooker and Waters, but he doubted "that more than a few thousand white Americans outside the Deep South have ever heard B. B. King's music."

Blues-rock

By the time Keil's book appeared, the situation he described was changing dramatically. Thanks in a large part to the "British invasion" that followed the Beatles' arrival in the United States, young listeners were seeing less and less reason to draw strict lines between folk-blues revivalism and crowd-pleasing rock 'n' roll. The Rolling Stones, Eric Clapton, John Mayall, the Yardbirds, and the Animals were hardcore blues aficionados, but they also sold millions of records. They were matched by Americans including the Paul Butterfield Blues Band, Canned Heat, the Blues Project, and, by the end of the decade, Janis Joplin and Jimi Hendrix. Many of these performers were particularly devoted to the down-home Chicago style, and they inspired a new audience to seek out Muddy Waters and Howlin' Wolf, who responded by recording in London with casts of British sidemen and releasing "psychedelic" LPs aimed at the rock market. Others, notably Clapton and Hendrix, were inspired by the instrumental virtuosity of B. B. King and the guitarists whose styles flowed from his innovations, including the unrelated Albert and Freddy King. (Clapton was immersed in older styles as well, consistently naming Robert Johnson as his favorite blues artist.) By the later 1960s all three Kings were sharing bills with rock bands at venues like San Francisco's Fillmore West, alongside younger Chicago players such as Junior Wells, Buddy Guy, and Otis Rush.

The overlap of blues, rock, and soul mingled disparate artists and audiences, so it is worth noting that the Kings reached young rock fans by different routes: B. B. was hailed as the "ambassador

9. Buddy Guy accompanies Big Mama Thornton singing her original version of "Hound Dog" during a concert in Germany on the 1965 American Folk Blues Festival tour.

of the blues" and tended to be appreciated as much for his deep roots as for his innovations. Albert, who had modified B. B.'s style with screaming, high-note string bends, became the bluesman for the soul crowd thanks to his contract with Memphis's Stax

Records. And Freddy, who had his biggest hit with a twelve-bar instrumental, "Hide Away," originally crossed over by appealing to the young dancers who were buying surf guitar bands.

Between the folk-blues revival and the blues-rock boom, by the mid-1960s blues was attracting not only new kinds of listeners but a new range of performers. The most successful tended to be young white American and British musicians, whether electrified blues-rockers or acoustic artists such as Dave Van Ronk, John Hammond, the Jim Kweskin Jug Band, and Koerner, Ray, and Glover. When acoustic and electric styles overlapped in a new style dubbed folk-rock, these two groups often converged: Van Ronk and Hammond had their most consistent success as solo, acoustic artists, but also experimented with electric styles, and Hammond in particular continues to attract a mix of folk, blues, and rock fans. Janis Joplin, by far the most successful woman to emerge from the blues-rock movement, started out in her native Texas as an acoustic coffeehouse singer. Taj Mahal, the lone African American blues revivalist to build a lasting career in this period, started out playing acoustic music in New England, then formed a rock band in Los Angeles with the guitarist Ry Cooder, and has since ranged from the oldest southern styles to rock, jazz, reggae, and collaborations with African and Hawaiian musicians. Even Jimi Hendrix experimented with acoustic blues on occasion, as well as briefly playing lead guitar for Hammond. And the blues-rock movement's most innovative and influential songwriter, Bob Dylan, started out as a purely acoustic performer on the Greenwich Village folk scene.

Dylan and Hendrix do not tend to be classified as blues artists, but both made blues the bedrock of their work. From his first album, Dylan drew on the work of Booker White, Big Joe Williams, and other old blues performers, and many of his early compositions employed the basic twelve-bar form. In his autobiography, he credits Robert Johnson as a prime influence on his innovative lyrical approach, praising "the free association that he used, the sparkling allegories, big-ass truths wrapped in the hard shell of nonsensical abstraction." And when he went electric at the Newport Folk Festival, rather than turning to the gentler approach of the Byrds and the Beatles, he was backed by members of the Butterfield Blues Band.

As for Hendrix, he grew up with the music of Muddy Waters, Howlin' Wolf, and B. B. King, as well as the rock 'n' roll that was hitting in his native Seattle. After working as an R&B sideman with Little Richard, the Isley Brothers, and Joey Dee's Starliters, he shifted to Greenwich Village's bohemian club circuit, appearing both as a soloist and with John Hammond. The Animals' bass player, Chas Chandler, brought him to London, where he adopted the psychedelic garb of the British art-rock world and also took note of the growing interest in Chicago blues. When he made his spectacular return to the United States at 1967's Monterey International Pop Festival, he opened with Wolf's "Killing Floor," and although he ranged far afield from the blues tradition—indeed, from any previous tradition—he consistently revisited blues forms until his death in 1970 and remains a potent influence on later blues players.

The innovations of these artists were carried in multifarious directions by later bands, including such disparate figures as the Allman Brothers, who pioneered a new southern rock style, Led Zeppelin and Jeff Beck in England, and even Black Sabbath, who made crunching blues-based riffs a foundation of heavy metal.

The blues today

Since the later 1960s, blues has continued to spawn new artists and offshoots, but the range of music that tends to be grouped within the blues category has changed very little. Blues is generally regarded as a "roots" style, defined by its links to older music, and performers have earned the right to call themselves blues artists by proving their command of historical forms and their engagement with African American traditions. As always, that is to some extent a matter of definition: R&B is still the standard music industry term for African American pop, from soul ballads to hip-hop, and though some young listeners may be unaware that those letters stand for rhythm and blues, they are a reminder of the continuity between past and present.

New performers have continued to mine the blues tradition, new audiences have continued to discover old styles, and there has been a flood of books, recordings, films, and Web sites documenting a century's worth of blues history. Later acoustic revivalists have included Paul Geremia, Rory Block, Steve James, and a wave of African American artists including Corey Harris, Guy Davis, and Alvin Youngblood Hart. Electric performers have ranged from Chicago-style, down-home players to good-time bar bands, including such popular performers as Robert Cray and the Fabulous Thunderbirds, as well as a few break-out artists whose popularity has led to them being filed in the rock category: Johnny Winter, Bonnie Raitt, George Thorogood, Stevie Ray Vaughan, and at the more recent and esoteric end of the spectrum, the White Stripes. Vaughan in particular inspired a new generation of blues performers with a string of hit albums in the early 1980s, and his style, based on virtuosic, extended guitar solos, has continued to dominate the electric scene and is probably what most young fans today first think of when they hear the word "blues."

As always, some of the most distinctive later variations on the blues tradition have come from artists who are associated with other genres. Hip-hop and alternative rock artists have drawn on blues sources in sometimes startling ways. Mississippi's Fat Possum record label, after issuing a series of discs by older blues players, experimented with remixes and fusion tracks pairing those performers with young punks and rappers. The North Mississippi All-Stars have made a more organic mix of blues-rock and studio beats. And Corey Harris, Chris Thomas King, and the rapper Nas with his father Olu Dara have made records that explicitly connect hip-hop and blues traditions.

Since the 1990s, as the rap scene has increasingly become dominated by artists from the Deep South, some scholars have argued that blues and rap should be seen as part of a historical continuum. Others fiercely disagree, but it is easy to point out examples of proto-rap in the work of everyone from the Memphis Jug Band to Louis Jordan and John Lee Hooker. And however one defines the forms, they clearly draw from an overlapping range of African American traditions and have shared somewhat similar cultural roles.

There has also been a resurgence of blues—at least as a marketing term—among older African American listeners, especially in the South and the urban Midwest. Artists including Z. Z. Hill, Clarence Carter, Denise LaSalle, Latimore, and Bobby Rush, on labels such as Jackson's Malaco and Atlanta's Ichiban, have kept the southern soul style of the 1960s alive by marketing it as a new kind of down home blues. Some of those artists came to call their music blues only after dropping off the R&B charts, but they have reconnected with twelve-bar lyrics and electric guitars, and they continue to work in the same regions and for the same societal groups that produced the earliest blues styles.

However one chooses to define the music, blues is still very much with us. And, in a way, the greatest strength of blues is that it has included and inspired such a broad variety of work over the years. Along with being a song style and a musical genre, it has been—and continues to be—a tradition, an approach, and a spirit that permeates virtually all American music, and the work of myriad artists around the world.

Part II
Blues in American culture

Chapter 4
Blues and jazz

Blues and jazz have been intertwined since before either style had a name. The first description of jazz music appeared in the *Chicago Daily Tribune* in 1915 under the headline "Blues Is Jazz and Jazz Is Blues," and when the first jazz record appeared a year and a half later, it was a twelve-bar instrumental titled "Livery Stable Blues."

Virtually all historians believe that rural blues songs were a significant source for early jazz, though what they tend to mean by "blues" in this context is any sort of moaning holler with obviously African roots. Blues phrasing—the tonal subtleties that sound slurred or off-pitch to European ears, and the relaxed command of intricate rhythms—has always been a hallmark of jazz, and some people have even insisted that it defines jazz. Others counter that specific tonal approaches are less important than a more generalized blues spirit. The pianist Billy Taylor said, "It's not the fact that a man on certain occasions would flat a certain note, bend a note or do something which is strictly a blues-type device. It's just that whatever this nebulous feeling is—the vitality they seem to get in the blues—…it makes the difference between Coleman Hawkins's 'Body and Soul' and a society tenor player's 'Body and Soul.'"

When early jazz musicians described the music of their youth, they frequently mentioned blues. Papa John Joseph, born in

New Orleans in 1877, recalled that the first brass bands he heard played both blues and popular numbers at dances. The music of Buddy Bolden, the New Orleans trumpeter who is generally credited with leading the first true jazz band, is usually described as a fusion of blues—the main African American style brought to the city by ex-slaves after emancipation—and the Caribbean Creole style of the city's earlier "colored" residents. In this context, blues meant not only a kind of song, but a dance tempo, the slow rhythm to which dancers did the "drag" or the "belly rub."

Many older players distinguished blues from "popular" numbers, by which they meant songs that were available in printed form. Some blues songs had relatively consistent lyrics and melodies, but many were just unnamed instrumentals, sometimes associated with a particular musician or band, sometimes improvised at a dance and never played again. Bolden had a favorite tune that is recalled simply as "Buddy Bolden's Blues," and it got to be so popular that in 1904 its main theme was turned into the first part of a ragtime hit in honor of that year's World's Fair, the "St. Louis Tickle."

Jelly Roll Morton's recorded memoirs suggest the richness of the blues field two decades before the first commercial blues records were made, and hint at how much was lost due to the limitations of those records. He remembered songs that used language as raw as anything in rap, and that were far longer than anything recorded by later blues singers—a twelve-bar blues "Murder Ballad" follows its heroine through fifty verses, as she kills her boyfriend's lover, has a lesbian affair in prison, and finally dies, advising her fellow inmates not to make her mistakes.

Morton said that in his youth there were many musicians playing twelve-bar blues in Gulf Coast saloons, and this may have been where that pattern jelled and became the most common blues form. In Biloxi, Mississippi, he visited "an old honky-tonk, where nothing but the blues were played. There was fellows around played the blues like Brocky Johnny, Skinny Head Pete, Old Florida Sam, and Tricky Sam....They just played just ordinary blues—the real lowdown blues, honky-tonk blues." The examples of this music that Morton played ranged from slow, moody pieces that sound like the roots of Leroy Carr's ballads to fast numbers with the repeated, eight-beats-to-the-bar bass lines that would become known as boogie-woogie. He also mentioned a New Orleans pianist and singer named Mamie Desdunes, who played blues flavored with a variation on the Cuban *habanera* rhythm, a mix that would reappear again and again over the next century.

When jazz became a national craze, New Orleans blues formed a huge proportion of its core repertoire. The Original Dixieland Jazz Band, a group of white New Orleanians, set off the jazz recording boom with "Livery Stable Blues" in 1917, and its success spawned a flock of imitators, both black and white. Relatively few African American bands were recorded until Mamie Smith's success led to the creation of Race record lines in the early 1920s, and it may be due to the dominance of the blues queens that those bands' records include so much blues material. King Oliver, the New Orleans cornetist who led Chicago's most influential black orchestra in this period, devoted roughly a third of his early records to twelve-bar blues. Louis Armstrong, who came north to join Oliver in 1922, moved to New York in 1924 and introduced the New Orleans blues flavor to Fletcher Henderson's sophisticated ballroom orchestra. Armstrong's work with Henderson, especially on pieces like the twelve-bar "Sugarfoot Stomp," helped to make this band the main laboratory for the riff-oriented, ferociously danceable style that would become known as swing.

Henderson originally moved to New York from Atlanta to go to graduate school at Columbia University, and his background involved little if any blues. He began his musical career as the house pianist at Black Swan Records, which was named in honor of an African American opera star and intended to elevate the perception of African American music by recording classical and mainstream pop performers. In 1921 Black Swan yielded to the current trends by signing Ethel Waters, and she reported that Henderson was ill-suited to this stylistic shift: "Fletcher, though a fine arranger and a brilliant band leader, leans more to the classical side.... [He] wouldn't give me what I call 'the damn-it-to-hell bass,' that chump-chump stuff that real jazz needs." She added that under her tutelage he eventually mastered blues rhythms, but this story highlights the disparate strains that went into jazz, and the role blues often played.

Garvin Bushell, the clarinetist for both Mamie Smith's Jazz Hounds and the Henderson band that toured with Waters, pointed out that the problem was not limited to Henderson: "There wasn't an eastern performer who could really play the blues. We later absorbed it from the southern musicians we heard, but it wasn't original with us. We didn't put that quarter-tone pitch in the music the way the southerners did. Up north we leaned toward ragtime conception—a lot of notes."

The composer and musicologist Gunther Schuller has argued that without the success of the blues queens, jazz as we know it might not exist:

> It has never been emphasized sufficiently that the blues craze, following on the heels of the novelty-jazz fad, served to clarify the distinctions between a deeply felt musical expression of a certain ethnic group and a rather superficial, derived commercial commodity. In the process, the blues craze may even have saved jazz from oblivion. Perhaps King Oliver's Creole Jazz Band of 1923, and the subsequent efforts of Armstrong and Morton, would have saved jazz anyway. But already in 1922, the blues recordings of Mamie Smith and the hundreds of other girls who were keeping the recording studios busy were providing abundant evidence that there was a wide gulf between the blues and its attendant instrumental style, and the tricky slapstick music that was being passed off as New Orleans jazz. At the same time, the blues made

quite clear the musical distinctions between it and the commercial world of dance bands with their smoothly insipid saxophones and unimaginative stock arrangements.

Some experts would consider that an extreme position, but much of the greatest jazz of the 1920s was unquestionably made by musicians who played a lot of blues and worked with a lot of blues singers. Indeed, many musicians would have been hard put to decide whether they were primarily jazz or blues artists. Nor was that true only of musicians we think of as standing on the jazz side of the divide. Lonnie Johnson is remembered primarily as a bluesman, but he prided himself on his versatility and said that the only reason he became known for blues was that he won a blues singing contest at a St. Louis theater, which offered an OKeh recording contract as first prize: "I guess I would have done anything to get recorded … [and] it just happened to be a blues contest, so I sang blues." As a singer, Johnson made some of the most popular blues records of the 1920s and 1930s, but he also recorded as a guitar soloist with Louis Armstrong's and Duke Ellington's bands, and his superb tone and deft fingerwork inspired everyone from the white jazz pioneer Eddie Lang to B. B. King. Even the notably rural-sounding Texas Alexander recorded with accompanists ranging from the Mississippi Sheiks to Johnson and a New York studio trio of Lang, King Oliver, and the New Orleans pianist Clarence Williams.

It was a complicated relationship, with plenty of borrowing on both sides, and records captured only a small and not necessarily representative fraction of what was being performed. In 1937 Robert Johnson recorded a song called "From Four Until Late," which seems to blend his Delta style with the smoother approach of Piedmont singer-guitarists like Blind Blake—but the same song had been published and recorded fifteen years earlier by a Memphis trumpeter named Johnny Dunn, the leader of Mamie Smith's Jazz Hounds. There is no way to know whether Dunn was playing an older song he had heard from a country guitarist or Johnson had learned it from jazz musicians in Memphis, and in either case this is an example of an intimate and ongoing overlap. Two of Johnson's occasional partners, Johnny Shines and Honeyboy Edwards, recalled working with pianists and horn players and performing jazz standards—though neither recorded anything but blues—and Johnson's protégé Robert Lockwood helped reshape Chicago blues guitar by injecting a chord sense developed in jazz-oriented combos.

Meanwhile, in Kansas City, a generation of jazz-blues artists was transforming American dance music. The city's most popular bandleader, Bennie Moten, made his record debut in 1923 with a twelve-bar blues called "Elephant's Wobble," and in 1929 and 1930 he added a group of players from an even more blues-oriented rival band, Walter Page's Blue Devils, which included singer Jimmy Rushing and pianist William "Count" Basie. Basie was from New Jersey and had been a protégé of Fats Waller, one of the greatest stride pianists in the New York style. Waller had terrific swing but no discernable blues feeling, and Basie noted in his autobiography that although he had heard the blues queens, he "hadn't got my first real taste of the blues" until he arrived in Kansas City. Once there, Basie absorbed the local variation of King Oliver's New Orleans–Chicago style; by the time he first recorded as a bandleader in 1936/37, he had stripped down Waller's flashy piano technique to a bare minimum of well-placed rhythmic accents, and was spurring the most blues-oriented big band of the swing era.

The Basie orchestra and its Kansas City competitors were not limited to blues, but their emphasis on blues forms and phrasing set them apart from the eastern dance orchestras. Basie's theme song, "One O'Clock Jump," was a textbook on how to swing the twelve-bar pattern, using a mix of older devices: boogie-woogie piano, call-and-response horn section riffs, voice-like saxophone solos, and a distinctive theme adapted from Waller. And as that arrangement was being picked up by swing orchestras across the country, the Basie band was also getting hits with Rushing's slow, soulful blues vocals.

In 1938 the record producer John Hammond (father of the blues performer) brought Basie east and featured him in the groundbreaking "From Spirituals to Swing" concert at Carnegie Hall. Along with introducing New York audiences to Big Bill Broonzy, the North Carolina harmonica player Sonny Terry, and the Kansas City blues shouter Big Joe Turner, this concert also helped spark a national boogie-woogie craze with a piano trio of Meade Lux Lewis, Albert Ammons, and Pete Johnson. The Tommy Dorsey big band had one of its biggest hits that year with a twelve-bar blues titled simply "Boogie Woogie," and the style remained popular with swing orchestras from then on.

Between the Kansas City bands, the boogie-woogie craze, and the flood of rural southerners into the urban north and west, by the early 1940s blues had become an integral part of the swing repertoire. Chicago's Earl Hines, one of the most sophisticated black bandleaders—for a while, his orchestra boasted a full string section—featured singer Billy Eckstine on two huge blues hits, "Stormy Monday" and "Jelly Jelly"; Lionel Hampton had Dinah Washington; and the white Freddie Slack band had the Washington-flavored Ella Mae Morse. In 1944 the *Chicago Defender* wrote:

> Time was when only California and the solid south gave two hoots for the blues—and then only the Negro populace of those sectors did the raving. The rest of the world was swing conscious. Today that is far from true. Such bands as Louis Jordan, Sam Price, Count Basie (the latter plays both swing and blues), Buddy Johnson and Jay McShann are favorites in every section. They prove it by drawing more patrons into theaters and dance halls and selling more records than any other band or bands....Yes, it looks like we are headed the way Ida Cox, Ma Rainey, Bessie Smith, Mamie Smith and others started us years ago.

Though some of the band blues hits featured modern queens, this time around there were plenty of male singers as well, notably midwestern "shouters" like Rushing, Turner, Wynonie Harris, and McShann's Walter Brown.

In terms of jazz history, McShann's most important blues stylist was not Brown but his alto saxophonist, Charlie Parker. A Kansas City native, Parker was just eighteen when he first joined McShann's "territory band" in 1938. ("Territory bands" were groups that were not nationally famous but did well in their home region.) Parker soon left for New York, and by the time he rejoined McShann two years later he was experimenting with a new approach to harmony, which would change virtually all later jazz. This approach was first preserved on record in 1941, when Parker introduced Brown's vocal on "Hootie Blues" with a floating twelve-bar solo that showed his debt to the Basie band's Lester Young, but also his innovative departures from that model.

McShann's band played the standard range of swing and pop styles, but for recording purposes it was strictly a blues outfit, and as a result our early glimpses of the most important musician in postwar jazz are largely in this context—though in the 1990s some live recordings surfaced that show the band's broader capabilities. By contrast, many northeastern players who joined Parker in the modernist style that was dubbed be-bop showed little affinity for blues, and the fact that audiences tended to prefer bands like McShann's and Louis Jordan's to their more musically adventurous groups just increased the disdain they felt for the straightforward blues stylists. As Parker's frequent collaborator Dizzy Gillespie, who came from an eastern swing background, wrote: "The bebop musicians didn't like to play the blues.... They'd play the twelve-bar outline of the blues, but they wouldn't blues it up like the older guys they considered unsophisticated. They busied themselves making [chord] changes, a thousand changes in one bar.... Those guys overlooked the fact that Charlie Parker personified the blues idiom. When he played the blues, he was a real blueser."

10. Charlie Parker was known for his dazzling speed and harmonic innovations, but he always came back to the basic twelve-bar blues.

Indeed, roughly a quarter of Parker's records feature twelve-bar blues, and along with his innovative improvisations showed his appreciation for the older midwestern styles. On his first recording session as a bandleader, made in 1945 with Gillespie on piano and a young Miles Davis on trumpet, two of the five tunes were blues. And, though bop was generally regarded as the hyper-intellectual antithesis of the dance-oriented rhythm and blues scene, one of the tunes from that session re-emerged as a huge R&B hit: Parker's "Now's the Time" thrilled modernists with the quirky, off-kilter harmonies of its improvisations, but the opening section was a catchy twelve-bar riff chorus in the classic Kansas City bag. Reworked by Lucky Millinder's big band as "D Natural

Blues," it was picked up by a sax player named Paul Williams, renamed "The Huckle-Buck," and turned into the biggest R&B hit of 1949—covered by everyone from West Coast blues combos to Frank Sinatra.

This continuing cross-fertilization was obscured by the internal battles of the jazz world. In the 1940s and 1950s jazz fans split into warring camps, some sticking to the old New Orleans style, some favoring swing, and some welcoming the modernists. Bop fans emphasized the artistic and intellectual strengths of their heroes by contrasting them with the shallow commercialism of hit makers like Millinder and Williams, while their enemies disparaged bop for cutting modern jazz off from its roots in dance rhythms and African American popular culture. As a result, neither group was much inclined to connect bop and blues. But unlike critics and fans, musicians—particularly working-class musicians—are rarely purists. Big Jay McNeely took informal lessons from Parker, led a teen band in Los Angeles that included the bop legends Sonny Criss and Hampton Hawes, and made his first hit record with a group whose trombonist was his friend Britt Woodman, later a celebrated sideman with Charles Mingus—but that hit was "Deacon's Hop," a twelve-bar showcase for the "honking" R&B sax style.

The fact that players like McNeely are remembered as R&B musicians while his friends are remembered as modern jazz artists is due to choices that were not always clear-cut at the time. If one compares "Tiny's Tempo," a twelve-bar blues recorded by the electric guitarist Tiny Grimes in 1944 with Parker on alto, with "Come Back to Me, Baby," recorded the following year by T-Bone Walker, the soloists take quite different approaches but the bands are clearly coming out of overlapping worlds. And as modern jazz increasingly came to be regarded as an art music, respected by intellectuals but not attracting dancers or heard on hit-centered radio shows, some young African American jazz musicians tried to reforge the music's links to blues, both for commercial reasons and because they wanted to remain relevant to their peers. In the 1950s a "hard bop" style emerged, rooting its rhythmic and harmonic experiments in older blues and gospel styles. The hard bop approach is exemplified by compositions such as "Doodlin'," a twelve-bar blues recorded in 1954 by the Horace Silver–Art Blakey Jazz Messengers, which was shortly covered by numerous other artists, including Ray Charles.

Charles provided a particularly obvious link between jazz and blues. His record label, Atlantic, was noted both for its radio-friendly R&B singles and its adventurous jazz LPs, and by the mid-1950s he was interspersing vocal-driven R&B hits with instrumental jazz albums, including two with Milt Jackson of the Modern Jazz Quartet. A musical omnivore, Charles could range comfortably from Leroy Carr's style to songs by Cole Porter and Hank Williams, but his instrumental jazz excursions were overwhelmingly based on blues progressions, and his first duet with Jackson was a nine-minute jam on Carr's "How Long, How Long Blues."

Such collaborations served the interests of both jazz and R&B artists, since they made jazz more acceptable to the young pop audience and R&B more acceptable to upscale jazz fans. The efforts to bridge that divide took many forms: Though most of the hard boppers were young African Americans, a white Mississippian named Mose Allison recorded a series of startlingly roots-oriented experiments that mixed bop-flavored piano with material drawn from Muddy Waters and Percy Mayfield. And at the end of the 1950s, Ornette Coleman became the most revolutionary and controversial jazz player since Parker with a style that reached back to the oldest African American traditions. Coleman was born in 1930 in Fort Worth, Texas, and though he worshipped Parker he got his professional start playing honking sax with R&B bands. He traveled to Los Angeles in 1950 with the Texas blues guitarist Pee Wee Crayton, though Crayton found his playing so weird that by the end of the tour he was not being

allowed to solo. Indeed, Coleman was considered something of
an oddball by his early peers, sporting long hair and a beard in
the 1940s and playing music that was farther "out" than anything
on record. In Los Angeles, he finally found a few musicians who
appreciated his unique vision and formed a quartet that pioneered
what came to be called "free jazz," abandoning regular chords,
rhythms, and melodies. This group's 1959 LP, *The Shape of Jazz to
Come*, still sounds modern half a century later, but it also shows
Coleman's deep roots: his playing has the raw timbre and non-
western tonalities that were common to Texas Alexander and the
Delta singers. Robert Palmer, the author of *Deep Blues*, wrote of
the reverence with which Coleman and his bandmates greeted
Robert Johnson's *King of the Delta Blues Singers*: "When the music
was over, nobody said anything for a while, and then Ornette said,
wistfully, 'I wish we could play the blues more like *that*.'"

That desire to reconnect with earlier African American styles was
an important factor in the jazz world of the fifties and sixties.
Those were the peak years of the civil rights movement, and many
hard boppers framed their explorations of blues and gospel roots
as declarations of African American pride. At a time when the
most commercially successful jazz style was the "cool" music of
Dave Brubeck, young black musicians turned to older southern
sounds as a way of reconnecting the music to what was happening
on the streets. These efforts could be as heady as Miles Davis's
Kind of Blue, which mixed blues themes with modal improvisatory
techniques adapted from Indian classical music, or as physical as
Mongo Santamaria's twelve-bar Latin/jazz/soul hit, "Watermelon
Man," which made both the R&B and pop top ten in 1963.
Nor were those approaches necessarily coming from different
performers: Santamaria's hit was written by Herbie Hancock, who
that year took over the piano chair in Davis's quintet.

Meanwhile, the most popular blues-identified artists on the
national scene—Ray Charles, B. B. King, and Bobby Blue Bland—
were all fronting bands made up of jazz-schooled musicians. And

just as the young jazz players were forging links to blues, many of the most successful blues artists cited their debt to jazz: King consistently named Django Reinhardt as an inspiration, and Bland's bandleader noted that the singer's phrasing was modeled on the behind-the-beat approach of Basie's 1950s-era vocalist, Joe Williams.

Given this shared history, it is arguably misleading to discuss blues and jazz as overlapping or interpollinating forms rather than as one tradition that has been marketed in different ways to different audiences. Even when musicians themselves draw stylistic lines, the result can be confusing: The trombonist Fred Wesley, a stalwart of the Ike and Tina Turner and James Brown bands, defined himself as "a jazz snob...a bebop snob, specifically," but his example of that snobbery was, "To me, the best that music can be is a medium up-tempo twelve-bar blues in F." (By way of underlining that connection, one of Brown's biggest dance hits of the early 1960s was a twelve-bar blues instrumental, "Night Train," which had been a hit in 1952 for Jimmy Forrest, Charlie Parker's touring roommate in the McShann band.)

A list of blues and blues-flavored instrumentals that hit for jazz artists in the early to mid-1960s would include trumpeter Lee Morgan's "Sidewinder," Cannonball Adderley's "Mercy, Mercy, Mercy," and a string of singles and albums by the electric organist Jimmy Smith that included covers of Muddy Waters hits. Waters returned the compliment, at least by proxy: live recordings from the mid-1960s show his band warming up the crowd with versions of "Watermelon Man," Adderley's "Work Song," and Smith's "Back at the Chicken Shack."

Since the 1960s, both the blues and the jazz traditions have been mined for rock fusions, and artists such as Carlos Santana and, more recently, various groups on the "jam band" scene have brought blues, jazz, and rock together in ways that at their best illuminate all three styles. To the extent that one accepts the standard marketing categories, many people filed as blues artists have continued to explore jazz harmonies and instrumental techniques, while many filed as jazz artists have continued to explore the blues tradition as a way of connecting to their musical roots—for example the singer Cassandra Wilson, who has produced evocative reimaginings of several Robert Johnson pieces. But as both genres have increasingly become associated with specialty audiences, they have most often overlapped in the hands of revivalists, or at least of artists who see themselves as carrying on older traditions.

For more than a century, through a host of musical evolutions, the role of blues in jazz has remained surprisingly constant. From the first, it was seen as rooting the most celebrated or esoteric new sounds in a deep African American heritage. And modern listeners still judge jazz performers not only on their ability to create exciting, complex, and innovative music, but on an ineffable connection to the experiences, sounds, and soulfulness of the past—and still call that connecting link "the blues."

Chapter 5
Blues and country music

Among the vernacular musics of the United States, jazz is often placed at the opposite pole from country and western. Where jazz is resolutely urban, country's name defines it as rural; where jazz has been defiantly modern, country has been insistently nostalgic; where jazz has evolved a complex and sophisticated harmonic, melodic, rhythmic, and concert performance tradition that has led to its being hailed as "America's classical music," country is noted for its musical simplicity; and where jazz is associated with African American culture, country is overwhelmingly associated with the white—indeed, until the 1960s, the explicitly segregated—South. Yet both forms are inextricably intertwined with blues, and blues has provided a meeting place between them. In 1930, when Jimmie Rodgers was America's most popular country singer and Louis Armstrong the greatest jazz virtuoso, they collaborated on a blues record; and almost eighty years later, blues provided a similar meeting ground for Willie Nelson and Wynton Marsalis.

If country and jazz meet at the blues, it has played roughly opposite roles in the two styles. Jazz typically turns to blues when it seeks to reconnect with its roots, while country has generally used blues as an antidote to conservatism. A list of the great country blues artists—in the sense of blues singers within the country genre—includes many of the genre's most significant innovators: Charlie Poole, Jimmie Rodgers, Bob Wills, the Delmore Brothers, Hank Williams, Bill Monroe, Patsy Cline, Johnny Cash, Merle Haggard, and Willie Nelson.

From the outset, blues and country music were defined by racial segregation, and both genres' histories continue to reflect a segregated view of an intertwining musical world. Folklorists and commercial recording companies—albeit for quite different reasons—tended to create a picture of the South that emphasized the separateness of black and white traditions. Early folklorists were attempting to document the oldest surviving styles and trace musical roots, so they focused on African American music that still showed ties to Africa, and on European American music that had obvious sources in rural Europe. Indeed, through the 1930s many folklorists considered blues too modern a style to be worth studying in either community. When the first comprehensive survey of African American rural folk music, *The Negro and His Songs*, was published in 1925, the authors concentrated on the most archaic-sounding material, gave secondary attention to songs that rural singers had "modified or adapted" from white or Tin Pan Alley sources, and did their best to avoid what they regarded as purely commercial forms, including blues.

The commercial record companies had a quite different agenda, since they were looking for salable lines of merchandise. But they quickly concluded that "Race" and "hillbilly" styles appealed to different markets. One difference was that white southerners were eager to buy music that recalled the past: The first country record lines were marketed as "Old Familiar Tunes" or "Old-Time Tunes" and concentrated on styles that reached back at least to the nineteenth century. Black rural southerners, by contrast, overwhelmingly favored music that suggested a freer, less constricting world than the one they had grown up in—for example, the bright lights of Memphis's Beale Street and the booming black neighborhoods of Harlem and Chicago.

One result of this cultural split was that some records of older-sounding African American artists seem to have appealed principally to white consumers. Collectors searching the South for vintage 78s have reported that Mississippi John Hurt's records were often found in white homes—and, as it happens, Hurt was originally recorded on the recommendation of a white fiddler, W. H. Narmour, who sometimes hired him as a back-up guitarist. Despite segregation, Afro- and Euro-American string bands played a largely overlapping repertoire and sometimes performed in mixed groups. (Many musicians recalled such collaborations, though only a few were recorded.) Fiddles of various sorts are common to both Europe and Africa, and by the turn of the twentieth century the old-world styles had been cross-fertilizing for hundreds of years. The official segregation of the record lines concealed this overlap, to the point that black performers who recorded fiddle tunes were sometimes sold as white hillbilly artists, even though the same players were marketed in Race catalogs when they recorded blues or ragtime.

In general, though, the practice of racially segregating rural styles led record companies to overlook black banjo and fiddle players in favor of similar-sounding white players. One result was that many of the older African American rural styles were recorded principally by white musicians—in particular the dance-oriented fiddle and banjo tunes, but also some material that was obviously related to blues. For example, in 1924 a white banjo player named Samantha Bumgarner recorded the generically titled "Worried Blues." The song's loose, meditative meter suggested roots in field hollers, and its structure consisted of four repeated lines with a concluding tag:

Going down this long Georgia road,
Oh, I'm going down this long Georgia road,
Going down this long Georgia road, oh, my love,
Going down this long Georgia road,
Oh, I'm going where I've never been before.

Variants of this song have been collected from both white and black performers throughout the South. Generally the first line is repeated only three times, and some scholars have suggested that the two lines and reply of the standard twelve-bar blues is just a further shortening of this pattern. By the 1920s, the three-line-and-tag form was already considered old-fashioned, so it was recorded far more often by hillbilly performers than by secular Race artists, but it remained common in the more conservative African American church tradition, and also in African American work songs. Robert Johnson's "Last Fair Deal Gone Down"—the most archaic song in his recorded repertoire—is a perfect example of the way this pattern can be traced to varying sources. It shares both its form and some lyrics with "It Makes a Long Time Man Feel Bad," a work song recorded from black inmates in the Mississippi State Penitentiary, and also with "Don't Let Your Deal Go Down," recorded by the pioneering white hillbilly star Fiddlin' John Carson.

When W. C. Handy's blues songs swept the country in the early teens, they were picked up not only by vaudevillians and urban dance orchestras but by white and black rural singers and string bands. The white banjo player Charlie Poole and his North Carolina Ramblers recorded sprightly versions of Handy's "Beale Street Blues" and the song Handy had adapted as "Hesitation Blues." Plenty of African American string bands were undoubtedly playing those same songs in a similar style, but their work was very rarely recorded. So groups like the Ramblers need to be taken into account by anyone attempting to flesh out a picture of the broader rural blues scene.

The blues queens likewise attracted a wide range of southern listeners, and white rural players routinely learned songs from their recordings. The Allen Brothers' 1927 recording of "Chattanooga Blues," for example, was adapted from a song of the same title recorded four years earlier by Ida Cox. The Allen Brothers were basically a hillbilly-hokum duo, featuring banjo and kazoo, and leaning heavily to blues and ragtime material. If the music catalogs had not been segregated, the Allens could easily have been filed alongside Papa Charlie Jackson—indeed, their first hit, like Jackson's second, was a version of "Salty Dog Blues." Apparently this idea occurred to someone at Columbia Records, which marketed "Chattanooga Blues" and its flip side, "Laughin' and Cryin' Blues," in its Race line and advertised it in the *Chicago Defender* with a cartoon of two black men. The Allens responded by threatening legal action, explaining in later interviews that this was not because they felt personally insulted, but because they would have been barred from white vaudeville if theatrical agents thought they were black.

As that story indicates, the ongoing interchange between white and black performers, and even the occasional mixed groups, did not imply an egalitarian relationship either in the musical job market or in society at large. Jimmie Davis, a country singer best known for the fabulously popular "You Are My Sunshine," recorded a series of wry double-entendre blues songs in the early 1930s with backing by the black slide guitarists Buddy Woods and Ed Schaeffer. In later years he boasted of the open-mindedness of this choice—but the players were hired strictly as temporary sidemen, and when Davis ran for governor of Louisiana in 1960, it was on a hard-line segregationist platform.

That imbalance of power has led some historians to treat white southern blues performers as, at best, imitators and, at worst, thieves, palely recycling a tradition that was not their own. More generous scholars have treated them as a parallel category of artists, contemporary with the black rural blues performers and playing a sometimes overlapping repertoire, but nonetheless belonging to a separate tradition. Each of these positions is reasonable in many cases: Some hillbilly players clearly considered their blues performances a sort of modern minstrelsy, putting on exaggerated accents and at times appearing in blackface. Others, such as Dock Boggs, a banjo player from the western tip of Virginia who created his own idiosyncratic take on the blues tradition in the 1920s, clearly came from a very different background and had a very different musical approach from the African American blues artists of his time: When he covered Clara Smith's record of "Down South Blues," his voice had the flat, nasal timbre typical of white Appalachian singers, and it was only many years later that scholars traced his source back to the Smith disc. In retrospect, Boggs's records are often seen as a forerunner of the "high lonesome" bluegrass style, but at the time they sounded archaic and regional, and had little if any impact on the broader blues or hillbilly scenes.

Jimmie Rodgers, by contrast, was one of the most broadly influential blues performers of the late 1920s, imitated by white and black singers alike. Originally from eastern Mississippi, Rodgers sang in a style closer to that of minstrel and vaudeville singers like Al Bernard than to Boggs's raw mountain cry, but what caught the attention of record buyers was his blend of blues and yodeling. This was not a new idea—his recording debut included a popular number called "Sleep, Baby, Sleep," that had previously been recorded by the African American "yodeler blues singer" Charles Anderson. But when Rodgers recorded the generically titled "Blue Yodel" in 1927, it changed the face of the hillbilly music business. The song was a typical twelve-bar blues:

T for Texas, T for Tennessee,
T for Texas, T for Tennessee,
T for Thelma, that gal that made a wreck out of me.

The rest of the song consisted of a grab-bag of older couplets— Jelly Roll Morton recalled hearing one about "going where the water drinks like sherry wine / 'Cause the Georgia water tastes like turpentine" (though referring to Mississippi rather than Georgia) at the turn of the century. But in the record market of the 1920s, blues was a hot, modern style, and Rodgers sang with an energy and humor that made "Blue Yodel" sound like anything but an

11. Jimmie Rodgers's variation on the blues tradition earned him the titles "America's Blue Yodeler" and "Father of Country Music."

"old familiar tune." A former railroad worker who was sometimes billed as "the Yodeling Brakeman," Rodgers conveyed the image in his blues of a rough and rowdy traveling man. To some extent this was a pose, which he adeptly balanced with nostalgic ballads about mothers and sweethearts at home, but he cannot simply be dismissed as a white imitator of an African American style. He was influenced by black singers, from the railroad laborers he had worked with in his teens to the blues queens, but his style was as personal and unique as Blind Blake's or Willie McTell's.

Rodgers spawned so many imitators and had such a far-reaching effect on southern recording trends that he is often called the "Father of Country Music." Indeed, he can be considered a one-man line of demarcation between the old hillbilly styles and what would come to be known twenty years later as "country and western." His most popular disciples included Jimmie Davis, Cliff Carlisle—an adept slide guitarist in the popular Hawaiian style—and two of the dominant figures in the country market of the 1930s and '40s, Gene Autry and Ernest Tubb, who both were originally marketed as Rodgers clones.

It is an oversimplification, though, to think of Rodgers simply as a hillbilly or country singer. He never attracted a large audience in the North, and to that extent fits the regional rubrics. But he was doing vaudeville tours at a time when most hillbilly singers were still playing for their neighbors and at local dances, and some of his recordings featured instrumentation that was clearly intended to attract fans of pop and Race styles. "Waiting for a Train," his best-remembered song after the blue yodels, was accompanied by Hawaiian guitar, cornet, and clarinet—a combination that pointed the way toward what would come to be called "western swing"— and other records used African American sidemen, including the Louisville Jug Band and the guitarist Clifford Gibson. The most famous of his interracial collaborations, 1930's "Blue Yodel No. 9," was accompanied by Louis Armstrong on trumpet and Louis's wife Lil on piano, reflecting both Rodgers's appreciation of the blues queens and his record company's apparent belief that he could appeal to a portion of the same audience.

Whether that belief was based on the numerous white fans who enjoyed Bessie Smith or on the numerous black fans who were buying Rodgers's records—or both—is not clear. But his popularity with black southerners was wide and pervasive. Robert Johnson sang Rodgers's blue yodels on Mississippi street corners, and the Mississippi Sheiks recorded a Rodgers pastiche called "Yodeling Fiddling Blues" in 1930. Of course, those efforts may have been primarily intended to attract white listeners. Johnson would certainly have sought tips from white passersby, and although the Sheiks' record was released in OKeh's Race line, one of their earlier discs had been marketed in the hillbilly catalog. Nonetheless, blues artists have often testified to their love of Rodgers's singing. Howlin' Wolf's falsetto cry has been cited by blues scholars as an example of surviving African vocal practices, but Wolf told the singer John Hammond that he got it from Rodgers: "I wanted to yodel in the worst way, and all that I could do was make a howl." B. B. King consistently names Rodgers as one of his favorite singers when he was growing up in the Mississippi Delta; Rodgers-style blue yodels were recorded by Tampa Red and later by the Virginia bluesman John Jackson; and when Mississippi John Hurt and Skip James got together offstage, they amused themselves by singing a duet of "Waiting for a Train."

One of the key factors in the popularity of blues across racial lines was that it was the only style that was considered both southern and modern. Jazz may have emerged from New Orleans, but in the rest of the South it was thought of as an urban—and hence, largely northern—style. Hillbilly music was marketed as nostalgia, to the point that when the Hollywood cowboys Gene Autry and Roy Rogers added studio-composed, pop-inflected styles to the hillbilly mix, these performances were still presented as old-fashioned cow-camp songs. Blues, by contrast, was both hip and down home, the sound of the honky-tonks and juke joints.

The Southwest was an especially rich region for hillbilly blues, for much the same reason that black southwesterners came to dominate the R&B scene. In both cases, the communities were less rooted and homogeneous, and hence less tied to older traditions, than rural communities farther east. In the 1940s black and white young people alike headed for California to serve the war industries. And in a further parallel, the western hillbilly scene included large dance orchestras, whose music became known as western swing, and small combos featuring electric guitars, whose style became known as honky-tonk.

Western swing was a hybrid suited to audiences who wanted to dance the latest jitterbug steps but also liked fiddle tunes, waltzes, and blues. There were audiences like that farther east as well, but in general they had to put up with bands that were good at one style and merely competent at the others. The western swing players were adept jacks-of-all-trades: When Milton Brown and His Musical Brownies made their first recordings in 1934, the selections included fiddle hoedowns, country waltzes; the Mississippi Sheiks' "Sitting On Top of the World," and "Garbage Man Blues," a rowdy twelve-bar rhythm number that had previously been recorded by black groups as "Call of the Freaks" and consisted of the band yelling, "Get out your can, here comes the garbage man!"

The most successful western swing bandleader was a sometime partner of Brown by the name of Bob Wills. Wills played fiddle, occasionally sang but usually just whooped encouragement to his sidemen, and by 1935 was fronting a twelve-piece band that mixed country fiddles with electrified steel guitar, piano, brass, and saxophones. The Texas Playboys, as they were called, were comfortable with everything from square dance tunes to the latest swing hits, and their instrumental blend allowed them to cover a uniquely broad range of blues, including material from W. C. Handy, Bessie Smith, the Mississippi Sheiks, Memphis Minnie, Jimmie Rodgers, and the Count Basie Orchestra.

From the point of view of later blues history, the western swing bands are also significant for being the first important groups to feature electric guitars. By 1935 Bob Dunn in Brown's band and Leon McAuliffe in Wills's were using electric steel guitars (played flat on the player's lap with a slide, in the Hawaiian style), and on some tracks McAuliffe also played an amplified standard guitar. The increased sustain of the amplified instrument allowed these players to imitate horn lines, and McAuliffe in particular seems to have been an early inspiration for the groundbreaking southwestern jazz and blues guitarists, including Charlie Christian and T-Bone Walker. McAuliffe's most copied slide solo was a twelve-bar instrumental called "Steel Guitar Rag," which the black slide guitarist Sylvester Weaver had recorded in the early 1920s as a gentle acoustic piece, "Guitar Rag," but now it had the power to cut through a full orchestra and established the electric guitar as a new kind of lead instrument.

As on the mainstream pop scene, the combination of amplification and the jukebox market meant that the large western swing orchestras began facing competition from smaller combos. Ernest Tubb had started out as a Jimmie Rodgers imitator, making his record debut with "The Last Thoughts of Jimmie Rodgers," sponsored by Rodgers's widow and played on Rodgers's guitar. But around 1940 a Fort Worth jukebox operator told him, "In the afternoons, when just a few people are sitting around drinking beer in these joints where my boxes are, they'll play your records all afternoon. But as soon as the crowd gets in there and gets noisy, they start dancing, they can't hear your records, they start playing Bob Wills." Tubb responded by adding an electric guitarist to his group, and immediately had one of the most influential hits in the country field, "Walking the Floor Over You," followed by the twelve-bar "Mean Mama Blues." Soon his combination of bluesy vocals with a small combo featuring electric lead became known as "honky-tonk."

Tubb's connection to the blues tradition came strictly from his devotion to Rodgers, but other Texas honky-tonkers were clearly listening closely to Race records. Cliff Bruner, whose Texas Wranglers was a cross between a small western swing outfit and a honky-tonk band, cut a version of Kokomo Arnold's "Milk Cow Blues" in 1937, a few months before Robert Johnson recorded his own take on the song. Four years later Johnnie Lee Wills (Bob's brother) made a recording of "Milk Cow" that established it as a honky-tonk standard, recorded by multiple artists including, eventually, a young Elvis Presley. Then, in the late 1940s, one of Tubb's followers took the honky-tonk style even deeper into blues territory, reshaping country music forever and attracting a fanatically devoted audience that spanned ethnic and racial lines.

Hank Williams was born in Georgiana, Alabama, in 1923 and learned the rudiments of guitar from a black street musician named Rufus "Tee-Tot" Payne. Like many southern singers who came of age in the 1940s, he was drawn to the western sound—even wearing a cowboy hat and calling his band the Drifting Cowboys—but his blues style owed at least as much to his upbringing in the Deep South. Where the Texans tended to treat blues as a rowdy barroom style, Williams wrote and sang some of the most mournful, heartfelt blues ever recorded. He could get hot and silly: his first national hit, 1947's "Move It On Over," was a twelve-bar boogie about having to sleep in the doghouse, and the song that made him a star was "Lovesick Blues," a yodeling novelty learned from the records of a blackface minstrel singer named Emmett Miller. The thing that made Williams not only a star but an enduring legend, however, was his talent for writing and singing soulful laments to love gone wrong. Not all were set in blues forms, but the blues influence was obvious, and African American blues artists have regularly singled him out as the white singer who most effectively made the form his own.

The late 1940s was a period of unique overlap in the blues and country scenes, in part because they were so intimately connected at the business end. Jukeboxes, the AFM recording ban, the population shifts of the Second World War, the arrival of television, and the new 45-rpm record format combined to break up the monopoly of the national radio networks and major record labels. By the late 1940s there were some two hundred minor labels in the United States, and many of them concentrated on niche and regional styles. Sid Nathan started Cincinnati's King Records in 1944 as a country label—its logo was a crown inscribed "If it's a king, it's a hillbilly." However, as he traveled around the South and Midwest, he recalled thinking, "Why should we go into all those towns and only sell to the hillbilly accounts? Why can't we sell a few more while we're there? So we got in the Race business." Nathan made a practice of acquiring publishing rights to the songs his artists recorded, and after branching out he increased his cash flow by sometimes having his R&B and hillbilly artists record separate versions of the same songs.

One of King's most successful acts was the Delmore Brothers, who had established themselves in the 1930s as stars of the premier country radio show, the *Grand Ole Opry*. The Delmores' style featured impeccably close vocal harmonies and crisp acoustic guitar leads, and laid the foundation for the later bluegrass sound. From the beginning they leaned to blues material, and by the time they signed with King they had formed a small band and were playing in a style aptly categorized by the title of their first King hit, "Hillbilly Boogie." In 1947 they added electric guitar and harmonica, and hits like "Blues, Stay Away From Me" established them alongside Williams as eastern hillbilly blues interpreters and laid the groundwork for what would emerge in the mid-1950s as "rockabilly."

The white country scene continued to be far more conservative than the R&B scene, with many listeners and programmers resisting innovations, and even the more innovative artists maintaining an explicit connection to older styles. Bluegrass provided a particularly clear example of the tensions between old and new. The music took its name from a single group, Bill Monroe's Bluegrass Boys, and Monroe was both a brilliant stylistic synthesizer and a bedrock musical conservative. As with Rodgers and Williams, he credited much of his style to an African American model—in his case a fiddler and guitarist named Arnold Schultz—and he had his first national success on the *Grand Ole Opry* in 1939 with a hopped-up version of Rodgers's "Mule Skinner Blues." As he honed his sound through the 1940s and into the 1950s, Monroe maintained a solid allegiance to the old hillbilly styles, resisting the use of amplified instruments or drums in favor of banjo, fiddle, and his own mandolin. At the same time, his fast, powerful rhythms and the precision of his arrangements gave his group a modern feel that inspired the same young southerners who were dancing to honky-tonk and tuning in to R&B radio.

One of those youngsters was Elvis Presley, whose first record devoted one side to a cover of "That's All Right, Mama," by the black Mississippi singer Arthur "Big Boy" Crudup, and the other to a reworking of Monroe's "Blue Moon of Kentucky." Presley's combination of white rural roots and R&B modernity was neatly captured in one of his early nicknames, the "Hillbilly Cat." His success opened a door for a generation of likeminded artists, from his Sun Records label-mates Jerry Lee Lewis and Carl Perkins to the Delmore-inspired Everly Brothers and the Texan Buddy Holly. But although Presley is remembered as a revolutionary figure whose shimmying hips and fiery vocals blazoned the triumph of rock 'n' roll, his musical heirs also include many of the most influential figures on the country and western scene.

As with so many genre divisions, the line between country music and rock 'n' roll was to a great extent determined by marketing choices. After Presley's success, it became common for white southern singers who showed a strong affinity for blues to be filed as rockers rather than country artists. There were some borderline figures: Johnny Cash recorded a few rockabilly discs but tended to be filed solidly on the country side of the divide, despite the deep blues sense that infused many of his best-known performances.

And in the 1970s a new wave of "country outlaws" appeared—once again, many of them coming from Texas—who had been weaned on Rodgers, Wills, Williams, Cash, and Presley. Waylon Jennings and Willie Nelson established themselves as powerful, distinctive blues stylists, and Tompall Glaser hired two of Bobby Blue Bland's sidemen in an attempt to break down the generic barriers between white and black styles. Meanwhile, Merle Haggard weighed in from southern California with songs like the self-explanatory "White Man Singing the Blues."

And then there was Ray Charles. After establishing himself as an R&B star with blues and gospel fusions in the mid-1950s, in the early 1960s Charles became one of the few African American artists to reach the upper levels of the pop LP charts—which had been generally hostile to both R&B and country and western styles—with *Modern Sounds in Country and Western Music*. Willie Nelson has often said that in terms of broadening the genre's scope and appeal, this album "did more for country music than any one artist has ever done." Charles extended that outreach by appearing on Cash's television show in the early 1970s and getting a number-one country hit in a 1984 duet with Nelson. Nelson has also done his best to keep the connection open in the twenty-first century, recording a blues album featuring duets with B. B. King, and one with Wynton Marsalis exploring the shared roots of country, blues, and jazz.

In a less race-conscious world, black fiddlers and white blues singers might have been regarded as forming a single southern continuum, and such collaborations might have been the norm rather than being hailed as genre-crossing anomalies. Indeed, it is arguably due to the legacy of segregation that blues has presented the most common interracial meeting ground, since, given a level playing field, many of the African American southerners we think of as blues artists might have made their mark performing hillbilly or country and western material. Ray Charles said, "you take country music, you take black music, you got the same goddamn thing exactly." And although that might strike some people as an extreme position, the sentiment has been echoed, often with regret, by numerous other performers. Otis Rush recalled that when he was growing up, Bill Monroe and Eddy Arnold were his favorite singers. The Texas bluesman Johnny Copeland was a fervent Hank Williams devotee, regularly playing Williams's songs for family and friends. And Bobby Bland told an interviewer in the 1970s that if it had not been for segregation he would have been a country balladeer: "I still know more hillbilly tunes than I do blues," he said wistfully. "Hank Snow, Hank Williams, Eddy Arnold—so much feeling, so much sadness."

Chapter 6
The language and poetry of the blues

Modern scholars tend to discuss blues primarily as a musical style, but much early writing about the form treated it as folk poetry. This was in part due to a long academic tradition of studying British ballads as the poetry of the common folk, and also to a growing desire among African American poets in the early years of the twentieth century to connect their work to a heritage other than the European literary tradition.

James Weldon Johnson, in the preface to his 1922 anthology, *The Book of American Negro Poetry*, wrote of blues as a new addition to the African American cultural heritage that had provided the United States with "the only things artistic that have yet sprung from American soil and been universally acknowledged as distinctive American products." Like most writers of that time, he regarded blues as a pop rather than a folk style—specifically, as a variety of ragtime. But he noted that blues songs were still being adapted and passed along in the traditional folk manner, and quoted some lyrics "that were popular with the Southern colored soldiers in France." One of these included the couplet, "I'm go'n lay mah haid on de railroad line, / Let de B. & O. come and pacify mah min'," which five years later would resurface in slightly different form in one of the most popular eight-bar blues hits, "Trouble In Mind."

Johnson apparently did not consider any blues compositions worthy of inclusion as poems, nor did the poets he presented show any signs of having been influenced by the style. But younger poets in the movement known as the Harlem Renaissance were beginning to claim the blues as part of their poetic heritage. In 1923 Langston Hughes had his first major success with a poem titled "The Weary Blues," which included what he recalled as "the first blues verse I'd ever heard way back in Lawrence, Kansas, when I was a kid." The lyric he quoted followed the standard twelve-bar form, repeating "I got de weary blues and I can't be satisfied" twice, then finishing the thought with "I ain't happy no mo' and I wish that I had died."

Hughes wrote numerous poems in blues forms, which he sometimes read with piano accompaniment, and over the years other literary poets have also dabbled in blues styles. The results have been mixed, since affection for the blues form does not mean that even a very talented literary poet can use it with the ease and brilliance of the best songwriters in the tradition. But blues phrases and inflections have continued to be a potent inspiration for many American writers.

The richest strain of blues poetry, though, has come from artists who with few exceptions did not think of their work in those terms. It is always tricky to talk about "folk" styles, but the blues tradition has been particularly open to trading, borrowing, repeating, imitating, and rewriting of phrases, lines, and verses. There is thus some justification for the early scholars who treated blues as a common language of African American singers from the rural South rather than concentrating on particular composers. This approach must be used with caution, since it risks underrating the importance of, distinctive lyricists such as Ida Cox, Leroy Carr, Lightnin' Hopkins, and Willie Dixon. But it is consistent with the fact that, especially in the early years of the genre, blues lyrics were widely regarded as common property, and even the most talented songwriters frequently employed sections of previous songs.

Most of the great blues artists were capable of composing original, cohesive lyrics when necessary, but in practice they often did not think of blues in terms of composition. They would simply play and sing, often for twenty minutes or more without a break, and the lyrical portion of the performance would be an impromptu mix of "floating verses"—couplets heard from other singers, many of which were common throughout the South—with an admixture of original lines, sometimes improvised on the spot. When such performances were preserved on record, it gave them a permanence that tempts us to think of them as finished compositions. But in many cases the singers would not have performed the same verses in the same order even five minutes later, and in general such "songs" do not have the linear cohesiveness of literary creations or narrative ballads. They typically start with a verse that establishes a mood or situation, followed by verses that may expand on that theme but also may veer off on apparently unconnected tangents, according to the singer's whim or stream of consciousness. Performers such as Lemon Jefferson and Charlie Patton frequently assembled songs in this way, and blues scholars have fiercely disagreed about the degree of randomness of the verses on particular recordings.

Other performances by early blues artists display an internal lyrical logic that makes it easy to think of them as poems in the formal, literary sense of the term. For example, in 1927 a New Orleans singer and guitarist named Richard "Rabbit" Brown recorded a twelve-bar blues titled "James Alley"—apparently after the street where he lived—and although it may simply be a three-minute anthology of favorite verses, on the printed page it has the measured flow of a planned composition:

Times ain't now nothing like they used to be,
Oh, times ain't now nothing like they used to be,
And I'm telling you all the truth, oh, take it from me.

I done seen better days but I'm putting up with these,
I done seen better days but I'm putting up with these,
I could have a much better time, but these girls now is so hard to please.

'Cause I was born in the country, she thinks I'm easy to rule,
'Cause I was born in the country, she thinks I'm easy to rule,
She try to hitch me to her wagon, she want to drive me like a mule.

You know I bought some groceries and I paid the rent,
Yes, I buy some groceries and I pay the rent,
She tried to make me wash her clothes, but I got good common sense.

I said if you don't want me, why don't you tell me so?
You know, if you don't want me, why don't you tell me so?
Because it ain't like a man ain't got nowhere to go.

I've been giving you sugar for sugar, let you get salt for salt,
I gave you sugar for sugar, let you give salt for salt,
And if you can't get along with me, well, it's your own fault.

How you want me to love you, and you treat me mean?
How do you want me to love you, you keep on treating me mean?
You're my daily thought and my nightly dream.

Sometimes I think that you're too sweet to die,
Sometimes I think that you're too sweet to die,
And another time I think you ought to be buried alive.

Whether improvising in the moment or carefully composing a
piece for a recording session, blues singers drew on all the sources
available to them. Their lyrics employed rural maxims, urban
slang, the flowery language of Victorian magazine poetry—Robert
Johnson's "From Four Until Late" finds the singer promising that
when he leaves town, "I'll bid you fair farewell"—phrases from
the Bible, and lines adapted from British ballads. For example,
in the ballad of Gypsy Davey, which had been imported to the

United States by British immigrants, a lord's wife ran off with a troupe of gypsies and he ordered his servants, "Go saddle me my old grey horse, the black one's not so speedy / I'll ride all day and I'll ride all night, until I find my lady." Lemon Jefferson reworked these lines in his "Black Horse Blues," leaving out the lords, ladies, and gypsies, but singing, "Go get my black horse, saddle up my grey mare, / I'm going after my good gal, she's in the world somewhere."

The rest of Jefferson's song suggested that the girl in question was traveling by train, and one of the distinctive things about blues lyrics was their blend of older traditions and references to modern

"Go get my black horse
And saddle up my gray mare,
Going to get my good girl —
She's in the world somewhere."

BLIND Lemon Jefferson, that famous down-home Blues singer from down-Dallas-way, and his guitar, have gone to work and made a record that will almost make your phonograph trot. "Black Horse Blues" it is, Paramount No. 12367, and you can get it now at your dealer's, or send us the coupon.

[12367—**Black Horse Blues** and **Corrina Blues,**]
Blind Lemon Jefferson and His Guitar.

12. Blind Lemon Jefferson, "that famous down-home Blues singer from down-Dallas-way," sings a verse adapted from an old British ballad.

events and technologies. Kokomo Arnold's "Sissy Man Blues" (which took its title from a joking reference to homosexuality), echoed Jefferson's second line, but abandoned the horse in favor of the telephone: "I'm gonna ring up China, see can I find my good gal over there / Since the good book tells me that I got a good gal in the world somewhere." And in 1936, a year after Mussolini's invasion of Ethiopia and the formation of an independent government in the Philippines excited widespread coverage in the African American press, Robert Johnson extended Arnold's geographical fantasy, singing: "I'm gonna call up China, see if my good girl's over there, / If I can't find her on Philippines island, she must be in Ethiopia somewhere."

As that lyrical lineage suggests, even the greatest blues songwriters have seen no harm in reworking each other's phrases. As with hip-hop sampling, the idea is to create something unique and new by a combination of borrowing, reworking, and adding original touches—with the advantage that the early blues composers did not have to worry about "intellectual property" suits. It is not unusual for a phrase that blues scholars cite as an example of a particular singer's poetic gift (for example, Robert Johnson's "When the train it left the station, there was two lights on behind / The blue light was my blues, and the red light was my mind") to be found on further study to have appeared in an earlier song (in this case, Lemon Jefferson's "Dry Southern Blues"). Such recyclings may strike some readers as plagiarism, or at least as lacking originality. But there is no way to write a comprehensible sentence without reusing familiar arrangements of familiar words—that is what makes up a language. The genius of the great blues composers was in the way they put old lines together with new ones, creating startling and emotionally powerful images out of common cloth. In Jefferson's performance, the verse about train lights was just a pretty image, but Johnson placed it as the culmination of a story about following his lover to the station and watching her leave him, and followed it with the haunting tag line, "All my love's in vain," giving his song a poetic unity that Jefferson never attained.

As professional entertainers performing for a generally young audience, Johnson and his peers intended their material not only to move their listeners emotionally but also to amuse and excite them. Hence the frequent references in blues songs to modern technologies, and even commercial brand names—Johnson, Blind Blake, and Peg Leg Howell all sang about women with "Elgin movements," a reference to the advertising slogan of the Elgin watch company. Bessie Smith referred to a popular brand of straight razor, singing that if her man did her wrong, "I'm gonna take my Wade & Butcher, cut him through and through," and Tampa Red updated this line in the 1930s to suit a brand of pistol: "Gonna take my German Luger, goin' to shoot her through and through."

Such violent themes are common in blues, as they are in rap, and in both cases they are often greeted by their core audiences as displays of comic exaggeration—though this humor tends to be lost on listeners from more sheltered backgrounds. Ma Rainey sang "I'm gonna buy me a pistol, as long as I am tall / Gonna kill my man and catch the Cannonball," and Jimmie Rodgers added a note of exaggerated sadism to her second line, singing "Gonna shoot old Thelma, just to see her jump and fall." (A line Johnny Cash in turn echoed in his "Folsom Prison Blues," singing, "I shot a man in Reno, just to watch him die.") Skip James sang that if his woman wouldn't come when he called, "all the doctors in Wisconsin, sure can't help her none"—he happened to be recording in Grafton, Wisconsin—and when Robert Johnson covered James's song, he shifted the location of the doctors to the more amusing locale of Hot Springs, a health resort.

Another of Johnson's songs, "Me and the Devil" includes a verse that perfectly combines wry humor with a deeper sense of loneliness and longing. Once again, he had an earlier model: Peetie Wheatstraw had sung the wistfully sympathetic verse, "When I die, please bury my body low / So that my evil spirit, mama, now, won't hang around your door." Johnson changed this into a request to let him go on traveling after death, using a form of transportation that was still a novelty to Delta dwellers: "You may bury my body down by the highway side / So my old evil spirit can catch a Greyhound bus and ride."

Just as old phrases were blended with new ones, references to modern innovations were balanced by verses evoking country life. One common verse, recorded by Lemon Jefferson in 1926 and repeated with variations in dozens of songs, goes "Blues jumped a rabbit, run him one solid mile / This rabbit sat down, crying like a natural child." Animal characters have always been a staple of African and African diaspora storytelling, and such verses are arguably part of the same tradition as the Uncle Remus stories, with their protagonist Br'er Rabbit. Another verse, recorded by Peetie Wheatstraw, explicitly recalls the trickery employed by those stories' frequent villain, Br'er Fox: "Want to tell you baby, like the fox done told the hen / I've got something good to tell you, if you come roll into my den."

Other lyrics drew on images that would have been familiar to any blues listener, sometimes with startlingly powerful effect. Lonnie Johnson turned a barnyard commonplace into a bit of cynical urban wisdom, singing "What makes the rooster crow every morning before day? / To let the pimps know that the workingman is on his way." And Sippie Wallace, in a verse repeated by many later artists, sang "I lay down last night, tried to take my rest / My mind got to traveling, like the wild goose in the west."

Leroy Carr built much of his reputation on such meditative, late night musings. The opening stanza of his "Midnight Hour Blues," like Jefferson's rabbit verse, visualized the blues itself as an active agent: "In the wee midnight hours, 'long toward the break of day / When the blues creep up on you and carry your mind away." He followed the success of this song with "Blues Before Sunrise" and "When the Sun Goes Down," meticulously composed lyrics that helped establish a new style of blues writing (as well as potentially providing him with royalties by tempting other singers to perform his compositions). But although Carr's songs were more cohesive than most rural blues and formed a pattern followed by Wheatstraw, Robert Johnson, and hundreds of other composers, their poetic sense remained firmly grounded in the older tradition. And, on a verse-by-verse basis, the traditional style could be as subtle and evocative as anything Carr or his followers created. Blind Willie McTell's spare, voice-like slide guitar on "Mama T'Ain't Long Fo' Day" makes the record sound old-fashioned compared to the urban style of the 1930s, but its title verse matches Carr's finest work: "The big star falling, mama, it ain't long 'fore day / Maybe the sunshine will drive these blues away."

Although blues has touched on every aspect of its listeners' lives, the most common theme—as in so many other lyrical traditions—has always been romantic relationships. In keeping with the mood that gives the music its name, the vast majority of blues songs deal with love gone wrong, but there are also plenty of celebrations of lovers, both male and female. Gus Cannon tenderly asked his woman to "Put your arms around me, like a circle 'round the sun," and Tampa Red sang, "When things go wrong, so wrong with you / It hurts me too." Ida Cox sang "My man's got teeth like a lighthouse in the sea / And every time he smiles, he throws his light on me," a metaphor that suggests not only her affection but also the contrasting darkness of her lover's skin. A similar racial pride was expressed by Son House in "My Black Mama": "My black woman's face shines like the sun / Lipstick and powder sure can't help her none." Such lyrics provided listeners with affirmation that was very rare in other media, and Mississippi John Hurt was one of many singers who took this idea one level farther, arguing for the virtue of darker skin shades: "Some crave high yellow, I like black and brown / Black won't quit you, brown won't lay you down."

The original blues audience was hungry for lyrics that reflected its own tastes and experiences, and although it is tempting to celebrate the music's universality, much of the language and content reflected the specific experience of those listeners. Many were desperately poor and yearned for things that might have seemed commonplace to more comfortable listeners—children who had grown up wearing clothes inherited from older siblings or white employers grew up to be men who would proudly sing, "The woman I love, she's five feet from the ground / She's a tailor-made woman, she ain't no hand-me-down."

The prosaic ordinariness of such images is a hallmark of blues writing, and at times this quality of direct, unexaggerated observation lends almost cinematic immediacy to a verse. In Sleepy John Estes's "Broken Hearted, Ragged and Dirty Too"—a title that tells its story before the song begins—a series of small details highlight his dismay on finding his woman is cheating on him: "Now, I went to my window, but I couldn't see through my blind / I heard the bedsprings popping, and I'm 'fraid I heard my baby crying." Indeed, the directness of blues lyrics can be jarring even to listeners raised on rap: Walter Davis reaches the same conclusion as Estes by an intimately close examination of his lover: "Your hair's all wrinkled and you're full of sweat, your underskirt is wringing wet / You been doing something wrong...I can tell by the way you smell."

Over the years, blues has been both hailed and criticized for its unblinking treatment of sexual matters. When blues lyrics celebrate relationships rather than bemoaning them, it is often in terms that are a long way from the moon-and-June clichés of Tin Pan Alley. Memphis Minnie sang about her "Bumble Bee" who "got the best old stinger [of] any bumble bee I've ever seen," and her chauffeur, who "drives so easy, I can't turn him down." Big Joe Turner, in a verse of "Shake, Rattle and Roll" that was notably excised from Bill Haley's cover version, sang of a woman who "wears those dresses, the sun comes shining through / I can't believe my eyes all that mess belongs to you," and described his reaction with a winking reference to male and female genitalia: "I'm like a one-eyed cat peeping in a seafood store."

The range of sexual themes and metaphors in blues songs reflects an honesty about the complexities of sexual relationships that was missing from most contemporary literature. William Moore's "One Way Gal" started out by describing how his woman "treats me right and loves me all the time," but the example he gave was that she went out in the rain panhandling or prostituting herself to support him. Numerous blues queens described similar relationships: Ma Rainey's "Hustlin' Blues" began, "It's raining here and tricks ain't walking tonight / I'm going home, I know I've got to fight." Domestic violence was discussed openly by both men and women, with Bessie Smith in "Hateful Blues" outlining a gory fantasy of murdering her mistreating man, and Robert Johnson chillingly declaring that he would "beat my woman till I'm satisfied." Even in more cheerful moods, singers could describe relationships that were far from the mainstream clichés of domestic bliss: "Papa likes his bourbon, mama likes her gin," Ma Rainey sang. "Papa likes his outside women, mama likes her outside men."

Such celebrations of sexual freedom reflected not only the complexities and varieties of personal relationships but also the exceptional mobility of African Americans at the height of the blues boom. Blues lyrics often referred to the ongoing migrations of black populations with lines about how Michigan or California water "tastes like sherry wine" while Mississippi or Georgia water "tastes like turpentine," odes to "'Frisco town" and "sweet home Chicago," and celebrations of the traveling life itself. "I've got the key to the highway, billed out and bound to go," Jazz Gillum sang, "I'm gonna leave here running, because walking is 'most too slow." Clara Smith sang, "I'm a rambling woman, I've got a rambling mind / I'm gonna buy me a ticket and ease on down the line." And John Lee Hooker dispensed with the ticket, singing "When I first started to hoboing, hoboing, / I took a freight train to be my friend."

As the core blues audience migrated from country to city and from south to north and west, the world that had formed the original blues styles largely disappeared. Blues singers increasingly found themselves serving an older, more nostalgic audience, and often fell back on tried-and-true lyrical themes. Today, it is common to hear people mock the style's tritely familiar lines about how "my baby left me," and relatively few blues composers have managed to deal in an original way with the day-to-day lives of modern listeners.

If the lyrical richness of the early blues eras was not maintained by later writers, that is in part because the singers of the 1920s and '30s had a very deep well of unrecorded sources to draw on. But it may also be because they were serving a more demanding audience: through the early 1960s, blues was still primarily being composed for a mass listenership of black adults, who expected to find their lives reflected in the songs. Willie Dixon, the most prolific songwriter for Chicago's Chess label, set a new standard in the 1950s with songs like "Just Make Love to Me," in which the protagonist gave an innovative twist to a familiar theme by insisting that, unlike so many earlier blues figures, he did *not* want his lover "to work all day," "to wash my clothes," or even "to be true," because "I just want to make love to you."

Percy Mayfield, who moved from rural Louisiana to Los Angeles and was a salaried writer for Ray Charles in the early 1960s, became known as the "Poet Laureate of the Blues" for intricate lyrics like "Please Send Me Someone to Love," which balanced a plea for world peace and understanding with the modest tag line, "And if it's not asking too much, please send me someone to love." As with all the great blues composers, Mayfield could balance even the most desperate themes with wry humor: "Lost Mind," a song about being driven crazy by "a devil with the face of an angel," opened with the wry request, "If you would be so kind, to help me find my mind / I'd like to thank you in advance."

Just as blues music has formed a foundation for myriad other styles, blues lyrics have had an influence far beyond the genre, not only in the lyrics of rock, pop, jazz, and rap but in novels, plays, graphic art, and films. In 1985, the mythic protagonist of August Wilson's play *Ma Rainey's Black Bottom* declared that blues was simply "life's way of talking." And if the language of the blues is easier to capture on a printed page than the music is, a single chapter in a slim volume can still only hint at the breadth and depth of a tradition that, even by the narrowest definition, is still touching audiences and inspiring artists more than a century after its birth.

References

Chapter 1

The Lomax intercutting of Senegalese and Mississippi singers appeared as "African and American Field Songs," on the LP *Roots of the Blues* (New York: New World Records 252, 1977).

Charles C. Jones, *The Religious Instruction of the Negroes in the United States* (Savannah, GA: Thomas Purse, 1842), 266.

John W. Work, *American Negro Songs and Spirituals* (New York: Crown Publishers, 1940), 32–33.

W. C. Handy, *Father of the Blues* (New York: Macmillan Company, 1941), 33.

Chapter 2

"Still Tops," *Chicago Defender*, May 30, 1936, 11.

Chapter 3

The quotation about Billie Holiday is from "Boogey-Woogey Pianists To Head Show At Apollo," *Chicago Defender*, Aug. 12, 1939, 21.

Dolores Calvin, "Hampton's Vocalist On Hefty Side In Voice And Physique," *Chicago Defender*, Mar. 6, 1943, 19.

Arnold Shaw, *Honkers and Shouters* (New York: Macmillan, 1978), 299.

Howlin' Wolf is quoted in Mark Humphreys, "Bright Lights, Big City," in Lawrence Cohn, *Nothing but the Blues* (New York: Abbeville Press, 1993), 187.

Buddy Guy is quoted in liner notes to the DVD *The American Folk
Blues Festival 1962-1969, vol. 3* (Santa Monica, CA: Hip-O
Records, 2004).

James Brown with Bruce Tucker, *James Brown: The Godfather of Soul*
(New York: Macmillan, 1986), 6, 17, 18.

Charles Keil, *Urban Blues* (Chicago: University of Chicago Press,
1966), 79.

Bob Dylan, *Chronicles*, vol. 1 (New York: Simon and Schuster, 2004),
285.

Chapter 4

Gordon Seagrove, "Blues Is Jazz and Jazz Is Blues," *Chicago Daily
Tribune*, July 11, 1915, E8.

Billy Taylor is quoted in Joachim E. Berendt, *The Jazz Book* (Brooklyn,
NY: Lawrence Hill Books, 1992), 162.

Ethel Waters, *His Eye Is on the Sparrow* (Garden City, NY: Doubleday,
1952), 146-47.

Garvin Bushell, as told to Mark Tucker, *Jazz from the Beginning* (Ann
Arbor: University of Michigan Press, 1988), 19.

Gunther Schuller, *Early Jazz* (New York: Oxford University Press,
1968), 252.

Chris Albertson, "Lonnie Johnson," in Pete Weldon and Toby Byron,
Bluesland (New York: Dutton, 1991), 42-43.

Count Basie and Albert Murray, *Good Morning Blues*, (New York:
Random House, 1985), 7-8.

"'B' Not 'I' Has It Because The Latter Is Swing Not The Blues," *Chicago
Defender*, Feb. 19, 1944, 8.

Dizzy Gillespie with Al Fraser, *To Be or Not to Bop* (Garden City, NY:
Doubleday, 1979), 371.

Robert Palmer, notes to *Ornette Coleman: Beauty Is a Rare Thing:
The Complete Atlantic Recordings* (Los Angeles: Rhino Records,
1993), 16.

Fred Wesley Jr., *Hit Me, Fred* (Durham, NC: Duke University Press,
2002), 308.

Chapter 5

Howard W. Odum and Guy B. Johnson, *The Negro and His Songs*
(Hatboro, PA: Folklore Associates, 1964 [reprint]), 149.

Howlin' Wolf is quoted in Jas Obrecht, ed., *Blues Guitar* (San
  Francisco: Miller Freeman Books, 1993), 65.
Ronnie Pugh, *Ernest Tubb* (Durham, NC: Duke University Press,
  2002), 66.
Bobby Bland is quoted in Margaret McKee and Fred Chisenhall, *Beale
  Black & Blue* (Baton Rouge: Louisiana State University Press,
  1981), 250.

Chapter 6

James Weldon Johnson, ed. *The Book of American Negro Poetry*
  (New York: Harcourt, Brace and Company, 1922), viii.
Langston Hughes, *The Big Sea* (New York: Thunder's Mouth Press,
  1986), 215.

Further reading

Overviews of blues history:

Cohn, Lawrence, ed. *Nothing but the Blues*. New York: Abbeville Press, 1993.

Jones, Leroi (Amiri Baraka). *Blues People: Negro Music in White America*. New York: Harper Perennial, 1999.

Palmer, Robert. *Deep Blues: A Musical and Cultural History of the Mississippi Delta*. New York: Viking Press, 1981.

Wald, Elijah. *Escaping the Delta: Robert Johnson and the Invention of the Blues*. New York: HarperCollins, 2004.

Chapter 1

Oliver, Paul. *Songsters and Saints: Vocal Traditions on Race Records*. Cambridge: Cambridge University Press, 1984.

Southern, Eileen. *The Music of Black Americans: A History*. New York: W. W. Norton, 1971.

Chapter 2

Abbott, Lynn, and Doug Seroff. *Ragged But Right: Black Travelling Shows, "Coon Songs," and the Dark Pathway to Blues and Jazz*. Jackson: University Press of Mississippi, 2007.

Albertson, Chris. *Bessie*. New Haven, CT: Yale University Press, 2005.

Bastin, Bruce. *Red River Blues: The Blues Tradition in the Southeast*. Urbana: University of Illinois Press, 1995.

Broonzy, Big Bill, as told to Yannick Bruynoghe. *Big Bill Blues*. New York: Oak Archives, 2007.

Charters, Samuel. *The Country Blues*. New York: Da Capo, 1975.

Davis, Angela. *Blues Legacies and Black Feminism: Gertrude "Ma" Rainey, Bessie Smith and Billie Holiday*. New York: Vintage, 1998.

Edwards, David Honeyboy. *The World Don't Owe Me Nothing*. Chicago: Chicago Review Press, 1997.

Handy, William Christopher. *Father of the Blues*. New York: Da Capo, 1991.

Harrison, Daphne Duval. *Black Pearls: Blues Queens of the 1920s*. New Brunswick, NJ: Rutgers University Press, 1990.

Lomax, Alan. *The Land Where the Blues Began*. New York: Dell, 1993.

——— . *Mister Jelly Roll: The Fortunes of Jelly Roll Morton, New Orleans Creole and "Inventor of Jazz."* Berkeley: University of California Press, 2001.

Chapter 3

Charles, Ray, and David Ritz. *Brother Ray: Ray Charles' Own Story*. New York: Da Capo, 2004.

Chilton, John. *Let the Good Times Roll: The Story of Louis Jordan and His Music*. Ann Arbor: University of Michigan Press, 1994.

Cohodas, Nadine. *Queen: The Life and Music of Dinah Washington*. New York: Billboard Books, 2005.

Dance, Helen Oakley. *Stormy Monday: The T-Bone Walker Story*. Baton Rouge: Louisiana State University Press, 1987.

George, Nelson. *The Death of Rhythm & Blues*. New York: Pantheon, 1988.

Gordon, Robert. *Can't Be Satisfied: The Life and Times of Muddy Waters*. Boston: Little, Brown and Company, 2002.

Guralnick, Peter. *Feel Like Going Home: Portraits in Blues and Rock 'n' Roll*. Boston: Back Bay Books, 1999.

Keil, Charles. *Urban Blues*. Chicago: University of Chicago Press, 1966.

King, B. B., with David Ritz. *Blues All Around Me*. New York: Avon Books, 1996.

O'Neal, Jim, and Amy Van Singel. *The Voice of the Blues*. New York: Routledge, 2002.

Rowe, Mike. *Chicago Blues: The City & the Music*. New York: Da Capo, 1981.

Segrest, James, and Mark Hoffman. *Moanin' at Midnight: The Life and Times of Howlin' Wolf*. New York: Pantheon Books, 2004.

Shaw, Arnold. *Honkers and Shouters: The Golden Years of Rhythm & Blues*. New York: Macmillan, 1978.

Van Ronk, Dave, and Elijah Wald. *The Mayor of MacDougal Street*. New York: Da Capo, 2006.

Chapter 4

Murray, Albert. *Stomping the Blues*. New York: Da Capo, 1989.

Rosenthal, David. *Hard Bop: Jazz and Black Music 1955–1965*. New York: Oxford University Press, 1993.

Chapter 5

Escott, Colin, George Merritt, and William MacEwen. *Hank Williams: The Biography*. Boston: Back Bay Books, 2004.

Malone, Bill C. *Singing Cowboys and Musical Mountaineers: Southern Culture and the Roots of Country Music*. Athens: University of Georgia Press, 1993.

Mazor, Barry. *Meeting Jimmie Rodgers: How America's Original Roots Music Hero Changed the Pop Sounds of a Century*. New York: Oxford University Press, 2009.

Russell, Tony. *Blacks, Whites, and Blues*. Currently available in Paul Oliver et al., *Yonder Come the Blues*. Cambridge: Cambridge University Press, 2001.

Chapter 6

Charters, Samuel. *The Poetry of the Blues*. New York: Oak Publications, 1963.

Oliver, Paul. *Blues Fell This Morning: Meaning in the Blues*. Cambridge: Cambridge University Press, 1990.

——— . *Screening the Blues: Aspects of the Blues Tradition*. New York: Da Capo, 1989.

Tracy, Steven C. *Langston Hughes and the Blues*. Urbana: University of Illinois Press, 2001.

Index

Page numbers in *italics* indicate illustrations.